THE
AWAKENED
INVESTOR

MASTER YOUR FINANCIAL ANXIETIES
WHILE UNVEILING A CONSCIOUS PATHWAY
TO PROSPERITY AND TRUE FULFILLMENT

TIM "JAI" BAKER, CIMA® GFS®

To all who desire know thyself

Cataloging-in-Publication is on file at the Library of Congress

Paperback ISBN: 9798891094109

Hardcover ISBN: 9798891094543

eBook ISBN: 9798891094116

Any references to events, names of real people, occupations, or real places have been slightly altered to protect the identity of the characters. The important essence of the stories provided are real.

Front cover image: George Peters, Artist

Book design by Designer.

Printed by DiggyPOD, Inc., in the United States of America.

First printing edition 2023.

For further information visit:

www.LuminousWealth.com

To my adult children—Elizabeth, Constance, Nicholas, and Noah. And to my grandchildren—Hawke, Remington, Indiana, Banks, and Ava ... and those to be born.

This message I also send to all the children of the world—I wish you to know your light, to live your days honoring and sharing the light, to express the true essence of your nature, and to experience a life that pours from your heart and soul. Joy is your inherent birthright. Fulfillment on this heavenly earth is your willful destiny. Always be humble and kind.

The Creator gathered all of Creation and said, "I want to hide something from the humans until they are ready for it. It is the realization that they create their own reality."

The eagle said, "Give it to me, I will take it to the moon."

The Creator said, "No. One day they will go there and find it."

The salmon said, "I will bury it on the bottom of the ocean."

"No. They will go there, too."

The buffalo said, "I will bury it on the Great Plains."

The Creator said, "They will cut into the skin of the Earth and find it even there."

Grandmother Mole, who lives in the breast of Mother Earth, and who has no physical eyes but sees with spiritual eyes, said, "Put it inside of them."

And the Creator said, "It is done."

—A Sioux Story

Mind is the master power that molds and makes … and man is mind. And ever more he takes the tool of thought and shaping what he wills brings forth a thousand joys or a thousand ills. He thinks in secret, and it comes to pass … our environment is but our looking glass.

—James Allen

BEFORE YOU DIVE IN...

Get The Awakened Investor Assessment

As a bonus for being a reader of *The Awakened Investor*, don't forget to claim your free access to our behavioral identity assessment.

It will lay the foundation for a deeper understanding of how you make moment-by-moment decisions with money, relationships, work, and yourself! The report we generate for you will describe your unique persona and is a wonderful complement to the chapters you are about to dive into. Visit the link below or use the QR code to get access...then click the **SIGNUP** button. EnJOY!

When you are ready, find an undisturbed location for to 10 to 20 minutes while completing the assessment. Relax into the questions. There are no wrong answers.

https://discovery.dnabehavior.com/investor/
LuminousWealth/1581/704

CONTENTS

FOREWORD

"Your energy is your currency; spend it wisely. Invest it in
love, compassion, and self-actualization."

MOOJI

TIM BAKER'S BOOK *The Awakened Investor* is an overdue
breath of fresh air on how to look at money as more than a
currency and build a positive relationship with it, which puts
you at energetic ease. The book will act as a huge wake-up call
for you and your family, alerting you to what's called the wealth
management service model, a model that you should seek out in
order to get the life you deserve.

I have had the great fortune to know Tim professionally and
personally for the last ten years, and in many ways, we have been on
a parallel track for our 40-year careers. The key point we agree on
is that if you want to live an abundant life, then it is fundamental
that you build a positive relationship with money. For many, that
will require making major life changes because they have become
prisoners to money in some way.

An important perspective Tim conveys is that if a problem is
going to be solved, then a different level of mindset consciousness
is required than what created the problem in the first place.
The reality is that money itself, in terms of being a currency for
exchange, is neither good nor bad. Rather, the problem rests in how
you perceive money and allow it to operate as an energetic force
across all dimensions of your life; therefore, you must understand
the multi-dimensional nature of money.

In the case of money and wealth management, if you, regardless
of your level of wealth, want to reduce the stress caused by money
and live a meaningful life to the fullest, you need to think about

money differently. Tim is avid that building a positive relationship with money and the overall wealth management process needs to start with the ancient Greek philosophical principle of "know thyself" and with a greater level of money consciousness.

Both Tim and I agree that one of the systemic problems with the current wealth management industry model is that money is typically only treated as a liquid currency. That leads to the wealth managers being overly focused on generating commission revenue from transactions and only managing the liquid investable assets of a client rather than addressing the overall financial life needs of the client as a human being and helping them manage their other tangible and intangible assets.

Another important aspect that has largely been missing from the wealth management model is the importance of a person's mindset around money and how to help people build a healthier relationship with money. Your mindset about money and relationship with money are largely behavioral in terms of your unique life perspectives and biases as to what it is and how it is used. Also, money is an energetic force ever-present in your thought patterns. The reality is that science shows 95% of cognition takes place in the subconscious mind. So, as Tim points out, if wealth management is to succeed, your thoughts about money must be understood and positively harnessed at all times without fear, anxiety, or confusion.

Having financial wealth and a sound financial plan can remove one layer of stress about money because it gives you more control over your future. However, because the energy of money is a quiet yet powerful force always in your thoughts about every aspect of life, it can directly or indirectly significantly impact every life decision, interaction, and action. Or, if any aspect of your life or relationships is not aligned or resolved, that can result in stress, which manifests in how you deal with money. In some cases, money in its currency form may not be the initial root of the problem, but the problem will be reflected in terms of money.

By adopting a broader perspective about money, the wealth management solution requires you as the client to be guided based on clarity of your authentic identity, emotional centeredness, and an enhanced relationship with money.

With this perspective, it is all the more important that the wealth management model you buy into must be based on a higher level of behavioral and money consciousness. Importantly, your wealth manager must have experienced this level of enlightenment themselves to take you and your family on that journey.

Since 1996, when I formed Coddington Financial Services in Sydney, Australia, one of my missions has been to help lead the development of a client-centered wealth management model that is holistic in nature, starting with "know thyself" and providing a customized experience for the client investor and their family, yet is profitable for the provider. Undoubtedly, I was a pioneer in trying this model on, and fortunately, enough people bought into it.

However, my greater love and purpose of self-empowering people globally with increased behavior and money consciousness rather than managing investments eventually took me on a tangential journey of founding DNA Behavior in 2001. DNA Behavior serves a range of wealth managers with online behavior and money insights, so they could go on this path of guiding clients to build a healthier relationship with money.

Since the mid-1990s, Tim has also been serving clients from the starting point of "knowing thyself" and having a greater consciousness of how money can cause stress in their lives. Tim is one of the few that I know who has completely gone all in on building greater neuro-money consciousness through meditation, heart coherence, energy management, and overall building healthy life equilibrium in every area.

Tim addresses the other important component of wealth management in this book: the need for a wealth management service model where a collaborative in-house team addresses every aspect of a person's life and financial needs based on their unique behavioral style. This is more than serving as a fiduciary in an investment sense. The service includes providing accounting, legal services, and human capital development from a central control point under one roof.

With the technology, tools, training, and coaching today, the right wealth management model can take you on a journey of obtaining greater joy, meaning, and health, enabling you to make quantum leaps in life rather than achieving linear returns.

Such exponential results can only come with a higher personal consciousness level and recognition of yourself as an energetic being.

Hugh Massie
Money Energy Pioneer
Executive Chairman and Founder, DNA Behavior International

INTRODUCTION
CONNECTING WITH
ABUNDANCE

If you can't control your MIND,
everything & everyone else WILL!
—JOE DISPENZA, RESEARCHER AND AUTHOR

WHAT HAPPENS TO YOUR BODY when you hear the word "money"? Even though you just picked up this book, I want you to pause for a moment and experience the physical and emotional sensations that arise from directing your attention to the word. Close your eyes, get settled in your body with a couple of deep breaths, and say out loud:

MONEY

Now sit silent for a few moments with your eyes still closed, letting the vibration of that word move through your body. Sensate what you are feeling.

I've been a financial advisor for nearly 40 years, and I often use this simple exercise when I meet new clients or speak to groups about investing. Some people report positive sensations, commenting that money has been a source of security, helped them achieve their dreams, or given them the freedom to live the lives they desire. If you're among this group, congratulations, and read on because with deeper awareness, you may be able to reach another level of personal fulfillment.

More often, though, the word "money" brings up negative sensations. You might have experienced fear, anxiety, confusion—even guilt. Believe me, you're not alone if you felt a knot in your stomach or a tightening of your shoulders.

Here's the important thing about these reactions: money is neither good nor bad. It's a neutral tool or a form of energy that can be harnessed for positive or negative purposes. If you had a negative reaction to the word, understand that the source of your stress is not money itself, but your relationship to money—the thoughts and feelings you bring to money, both consciously and subconsciously.

I want to show you how you can change that relationship. Doing that requires taking a step back and reconsidering some overlooked or misunderstood facts. Some of these facts are about the financial systems we have created. The wealth management industry as it exists today is a muddied landscape, fraught with conflicts of interest and disjointed strategies. I know! I have been blessed during my four decade-long career to have successfully managed the family wealth affairs of presidents and top executives of hospitals, private practice medical doctors, entrepreneurs, economic professors at major universities, and CEOs and key executives of publicly traded companies. I was trained how the insurance industry's watch was made, how Wall Street and Bank Street's watch was made and witnessed the birthing of the financial planning industry and its evolution. Then, I took my years of training and lessons to develop a client-centric multi-family office that became a luminous sanctuary to family wealth. With this experience, it's apparent that without proper guidance, this country's financial services landscape can be hard to navigate. In this book I'll show you the lay of the land and point you toward the people and organizations who are managing money the right way.

The other kind of facts I want to explore are deeper and more fundamental. In fact, they have to do with human nature itself. For starters, I want to examine how human biology contributes to poor decision making. Our bodies and minds have evolved over millions of years to be sensitive to potential threats. We experience fear when something seems to threaten our well-being. In some ways, that reactivity serves us well: it reminds us to run when we see a hungry lion. The trouble comes when we misinterpret situations as more threatening than they actually are.

For many of us, thoughts of money are like a glimpse of a hungry lion in our backyard. We immediately start to worry: Do we have enough? Will we lose what we have? Will we ever get what we want? We're driven by a sense of scarcity. Life presents itself as a zero-sum game, a fight for limited resources against others who have their own material needs to meet. Our fear makes us impulsive and blurs our vision. The world seems a terrifying place. And so, we make foolish choices—or we hide and hope for the best.

Meanwhile, fear (and its flipside, greed) causes many of our fellow humans to make unethical choices that threaten all of us. That generates still more fear, more bad choices—and more fear, more greed ... No wonder money stresses us out. We get caught up in our own personal cycle of fear, competition, regret, fear, and so on. There's no room for respite, for peace, for wholeness.

Not only is this stress emotionally painful, but it also takes a physical toll. After years of hoping that happiness or satisfaction will come if we just make the right move this time, only to find the cycle of stress repeating itself, our sense of *dis-ease* can lead to actual disease. Our health suffers along with our happiness.

This book offers a path away from fear and confusion to a place of peace and clarity. It's about learning to reshape our understanding of who and what we are, so that we can change our way of experiencing and participating in the world. Think of this book as a pause button that will help you to recognize negative behavior patterns, so that you can move forward toward the life you truly desire.

If it sounds like I'm pushing the discussion beyond the realm of personal finance—well, I am! I learned years ago that you can't solve a problem on the same level of consciousness that created it. I can offer suggestions for constructing your investment portfolio, but that won't change the negative sensations you experience as an investor or teach you to distinguish helpful advice from unhelpful advice.

MY PATH TO A LUMINOUS APPROACH TO WEALTH MANAGEMENT

Real change requires us to confront and examine the forces that shape us. That process can take many forms. For you, it might begin with reading this book. For me, it began in 1997, when I started a daily meditation practice. That work has opened my mind to the importance of living in conscious awareness and of how I choose to *be* in this world. I've learned, through the wisdom and guidance of incredible teachers and years of practice, to recognize the power of my own unconscious conditioning, and in doing this, I've come face to face with what it means to be human.

In 1998, I had the privilege of attending a meditation retreat in Wollongong, Australia with Deepak Chopra, the renowned author, physician, and teacher. One of his first lessons was to put all of us into pairs and ask us to whisper to the other who we were. A simple task, right? Most of us awkwardly said our names, wondering what the right answer was. Then he asked us to do it again—only this time, choosing another way to describe who we were. Then he asked us to do again and again and again … Each time, our individual identities expanded further into the universal: I was Tim, then a financial advisor, then a husband, a father, a son, a human being, a consciousness … until we were faced with the challenge of saying what consciousness really is. Eventually, we recognized ourselves as something more elemental—we are simply energy, vibration, light.

Beneath all our worldly identities, beneath our physical presence, we're all just light. It's an ancient spiritual concept that modern science has finally caught up to: all matter on earth—us, the plants, the animals, the rocks—literally came from the dust of stars. Quantum physics reveals that when we look closely enough, atoms themselves aren't even a physical form. They are just particles of light, constantly vibrating and flickering at a rate that makes everything, including ourselves, appear solid.

I believe that the path to an enlightened investment approach begins by looking at ourselves and our place in the world in a fresh, new way. Rather than operating as separate individuals— unconnected from even our neighbors and in competition with other people all across the globe—we can start to see ourselves as parts of a connected, universal whole. Rather than conceiving of ourselves as sealed off consciousness, we can experience our minds as threads connected in the larger cosmic fabric.

You don't have to be interested in meditation to find this insight useful. You might frame it in terms of other personal beliefs or spiritual traditions. But the implications are the same: the illusory world of scarcity, competition, and pain can, instead, be experienced as a world of abundance, collaboration, joy, and love. You can replace stress with gratitude and appreciation. And, yes, you can even participate in the financial system with a spirit and intention that allows you to live your life to the fullest while also sharing that fullness with others.

THE JOURNEY OF THIS BOOK

This book begins with a deeper look at the reasons that money generates so much stress and such negative outcomes for so many of us. We'll review the evolutionary and cultural forces I alluded to earlier—the ones that make it easy to fall into the cycle of fear, greed, and regret. We'll also examine the systemic factors that reinforce those destructive impulses—in particular, a small group of financial professionals with an outsized influence on how we think about investing.

Then, we'll turn to some common-sense solutions. The first involves becoming more mindful about your goals and decisions, so you can move forward with clear intentions. This step is about more than money—it's about your deepest, most authentic desires and how money can help you realize them.

The second solution is to identify and end the unhealthy relationships you've formed over time with people in your financial life, replacing them with positive, healthy relationships. We'll explore how you can experience this change when you work with a *fiduciary* advisory team who takes the time to truly understand the life your heart desires to achieve and acts solely in your interests. You may be surprised to find out how much is lacking in your current financial advisory relationships.

The third solution is to gain knowledge of our global Capitalistic system and adopt investment techniques that are firmly grounded in historical evidence and the current reality of the markets. We'll examine the research and reasoning behind evidence-based investing and why it makes sense for lifetime investors.

What's truly amazing is that when you revise your relationship to money in these down-to-earth ways, you'll clear space for an even deeper shift in your consciousness. I can't describe exactly how that will feel. You'll have to wait and see for yourself.

I'm in the wealth management business. Most people think of wealth as the accumulation of money, but the original meaning of wealth was closer to abundance. Abundance—true wealth—has nothing to do with piling up huge sums of currency or taking advantage of other people to get your share of the economic pie. It›s quite the opposite. It means discovering for yourself the inner light that gives you the freedom to express your unique talents and gifts for the enjoyment and service of others, to experience this world rich in health in a way that fulfills your soul, and to revel in the reflection of your joy painted in the world around you. When we live an unconscious, unquestioning life, we tend to blame external forces for our pain. But here's what gives me hope: we are not victims of outside forces; we are the products of our choices, and our choices can change how we experience the world. Bear that in mind as you turn the page.

CONTEMPLATIONS

- What do you feel when you close your eyes and think of the word "money"?
- Do you feel in control of your wealth and well-being journey?
- Are you always calm and confident in your day-to-day life with anxiety and stress only seldom and fleeting occurrences?
- Do you feel hostage to your DNA and the environmental portal you entered this life with? Or do you feel you can design your destiny?
- Do you place as much value on your inner world's journey as much as you do your outer world conditions?

PART ONE

FINANCIAL TERRORISM: WHY YOU FACE A CONFUSING LANDSCAPE FRAUGHT WITH DECEPTION

The confidence people have in their beliefs is not a measure of the quality of evidence but of the coherence of the story the mind has managed to construct.

—DANIEL KAHNEMAN, BEHAVIORAL PSYCHOLOGIST

CHAPTER 1

CREATING A RELATIONSHIP WITH INVESTING THAT'S ANCHORED IN TRUTH

To thine own self be true, and it must follow, as the night the day,
thou canst not then be false to any man.
—WILLIAM SHAKESPEARE

S IT POSSIBLE TO BE a successful investor without stressing out about the ups and downs of the markets? To not second-guess every decision about your portfolio? To face even the most fearsome recession with peace of mind?

It is possible. I know because I've experienced it myself and seen it in countless clients over almost four decades as a wealth management advisor—people who make investment decisions out of calm intention, rather than fear. People who create their own environment full of positivity and passion instead of reacting to what happens around them. People who don't feel isolated and helpless but connected and in control.

Most of these people didn't start from this place of peace and centeredness. More often than not, they came to me in a state of confusion, stress, or frustration. It was only after asking deep questions about themselves and coming to terms with the accumulated attitudes and habits of a lifetime that they could begin to change their situations for the better. It's not always quick, and it's not always easy, but it's a process anyone can undertake—including you.

What's different about a client investor who's made this transformation? The most important factor is that you know

3

yourself and what you want out of life. I'm not talking about the sort of routine goal setting that you might associate with a typical financial planning process. I'm talking about identifying your deepest passions. What do you most want to achieve or experience during your brief time on this planet? Maybe your passion is your family. Maybe you feel compelled to build community and fellowship with others. Maybe you want to sail around the world. The right answer is whatever you most desire—not what your parents wanted for you and not what most other people appear to desire for themselves.

Along with identifying your passions, the enlightened investor will have taken an honest inventory of who they are. They've acknowledged their strengths and weaknesses, and they've identified patterns of behavior that serve them well or hold them back. We all embody a complex blend of qualities, some of which enhance our journey, some of which create hurdles in our path. We all have a mix of positive and negative characteristics. But we also have the power to choose which ones we want to express. By embracing our skills and talents and becoming aware of our inhibiting characteristics, we can put the best parts of ourselves to work manifesting our unique desires.

Each of us has certain gifts that are ours and ours alone. Not everyone takes the time to acknowledge these gifts, but they're there nonetheless. Living well means nurturing our unique gifts and expressing them in our day-to-day actions for the betterment of ourselves and other people. Passion must be met with skill and action, which must be applied for the service and benefit of others. That's how to find meaning and fulfillment—and it's possible for each one of us.

There are a lot of ways to talk about this journey. You might have heard phrases like "following your passion." In the East it is referred to as "living your dharma." *Dharma* is a Sanskrit word that means "purpose in life," but with divine or spiritual connotations. One way to think of it is living in accord with cosmic law and order. "Living your dharma" means tapping into the part of yourself that's connected to something bigger than your physical body.

Where does investing fit in with all of this? We can't cordon off our financial pursuits from all the other parts of our lives. Instead, we can make sure that our investment decisions are helping create the world we want for ourselves and for others. Investing can enable us to live fulfilling and meaningful lives that have a positive impact on other people—in other words, to live our dharma. Rather than merely a means to accumulate wealth, investing can be an extension of our conscious awareness to honor the abundance provided by our gifts of creativity and service. It is powerful and transformative when trusted, rather than feared. It not only provides security for our lives but for the lives of others, related and unrelated. Perhaps that is why investments are referred to as "securities."

Even if everything I've just written resonates with you, you might have trouble with the idea that investing can be a spiritual activity. We tend to think of investing in purely material terms, and at its ugliest it can seem like a morally dubious activity designed to sort out the winners from the losers. But this widespread belief exists because investing—and Capitalism more generally—is misrepresented at every turn, from popular Media to misinterpretations of the Bible to the way we talk about it with our business colleagues, friends, and family members.

The Media presents investing as a chaotic churn of numbers that makes sense only to a cadre of insiders with special access to the inner workings of the markets. Turn on the TV at any moment, and you're sure to find talking heads going on about whether to buy or sell particular stocks. It's par for the course for two TV "experts" to recommend the opposite course of action on the same show, each presenting their case with equal force and equally compelling reasons. And as these people talk, you can watch the major stock indexes literally fluctuate by the second. This constant *volatility* stokes confusion and fear while reinforcing the misguided notion that investors are separate entities jostling for better outcomes than their fellow humans.

The problem with this picture is that it is entirely focused on the short-term movements of the markets, where publicly traded assets like stocks are subject to a nebulous force called "investor sentiment." That's just a fancy way of saying emotion. This focus on the short-term effect of emotions on stocks and bonds obscures the deeper truth behind the numbers that flash at the bottom of our TV screens—the truth that fundamentally, markets reflect and measure progress on the ground level of our economy, where human beings are inventing new worlds, creating experiences, and exchanging goods and services every day. This vast network of creation and exchange goes by the name of global Capitalism.

Finding creative solutions to problems, manufacturing goods that meet people's needs, providing services to enhance the human experience, and sharing ideas among the world's citizens— this is the heart of global Capitalism. Capitalism keeps moving forward, changing and reshaping the world regardless of what the measurement system (market prices) is doing on that particular day. And over the long term—despite all the short-term noise— asset prices reflect the quality of a company's earnings, which in turn reflect the creativity and success of human evolution and global Capitalism.

Capitalism has negative connotations for a lot of people. Why? Because Capitalism is associated with money, and money, as we've seen, comes with all sorts of negative judgments of its own. Probably the most prevalent myth about Capitalism is that it makes people greedy, that it separates the haves from the have-nots. In fact, it's not Capitalism that makes people greedy; it's poor programming of the mind and a disconnect from consciousness. And it doesn't separate us, it brings us together. After all, Capitalism is the work of individuals, and individuals can operate either out of fear and greed, or with awareness and generosity of spirit. Capitalism doesn't dictate the level of awareness of the people operating within its system. Like money, it's a neutral force—it's what we do with it that makes it appear either good or bad.

This point is easier to see when we go back thousands of years to the root of Capitalism. Humans first emerged as small tribes of hunter-gatherers, relatively isolated from one another and putting all their energy into procuring what they needed to survive. Only with the advent of agriculture, about 12,000 years ago, did humans begin generating a surplus of goods that allowed them to develop larger, permanent settlements where individuals could nurture unique and specialized skills. Some people excelled at sewing clothes, others at raising pigs, others at creating beautiful jewelry. To gain access to the full bounty of human creative expression, people began trading surplus goods with each other. First, they used a barter system, trading one good for another. But sometimes that didn't make sense. Maybe you couldn't trade a pig for a coat, for example, because the two things weren't equal. That's when people came up with currency, first in the form of metal coins and over time evolving into the paper and digital currency that's prevalent today. Currency helped usher in the age of trade between continents, connecting local and regional markets in a network that's grown into the system we recognize today as global Capitalism.

The moral of the story is this: Capitalism began with creative individuals exchanging the fruits of their labor. It's grown more complex since then, but at its heart, that's still what Capitalism is. In capitalistic societies, life isn't just about surviving—it's about thriving. We go to work each day inspired to solve problems and, in the process, change the world. When a whole bunch of people are working together to express their talents and live their dreams, there is a natural exchange that flows between everyone, and amazing things can happen.

Consider this famous example from the late Milton Friedman, American Nobel economist: the humble pencil. Not amazing, you say? Maybe you're not seeing a pencil in the context of the creative power of global Capitalism. When we go to the store and buy a wooden pencil, we're holding something we could never have created on our own. This small tool may incorporate wood harvested in Washington, graphite from Chinese mines, and rubber taken from a tree in Malaysia that was originally imported from South America with the help from the British government. Not only that, to cut down the tree for the wood it took a saw, and to make the saw it took steel, and to make the steel it took iron ore. Then there's the brass ferrule, the yellow paint, the glue that holds all the parts together. This seemingly simple object is, in fact, the result of thousands of people collaborating across the world, and what brought them together wasn't any collective decision, but rather the free market of global Capitalism. As Friedman says, the market not only promotes efficiency but creates a forum that "fosters harmony and peace among the peoples of the world. People who don't speak the same language, who practice different religions, and who might hate one another if they ever met."

This kind of exchange—thousands of people contributing to create something that didn't exist before—shows how pooling our talents and capital can help us achieve far more than any

7

individual or small group would otherwise be able to. It's natural for people to work together to solve problems and strive to make life more enjoyable for themselves and others. To do this on a bigger scale, they form companies, which in turn solicit support and grow bigger by borrowing money (you probably know these as bonds) and by letting people buy a stake in a company's assets and profits (stocks). Not all of these organizations succeed over time, but in the aggregate they do. That's because they're the collective expression of human vitality and ingenuity, and in this way, we lift each other up.

It takes time, but it happens. The late Hans Rosling showed in his 2018 book *Factfulness* that, contrary to most people's beliefs, conditions are getting better around the world. For example, the proportion of the global population living in extreme poverty has been cut in half in the past 20 years—but only 7% of people worldwide and only 5% in the US realize this. The other 95% of us believe that extreme poverty has either remained level or gotten worse. "Every group of people I ask thinks the world is more frightening, more violent, and more hopeless—in short, more dramatic—than it really is," Rosling writes. He attributes this misconception to our instinct to value stories over facts. Storytelling is a natural human activity that has contributed to the survival of our species—it's baked into our DNA—but our susceptibility to stories has also left us vulnerable to false and misleading narratives. (We'll talk more about this in Chapter 4 when we explore how financial institutions use stories to convince us to buy unnecessary and often harmful products.)

The fact is, in spite of stories to the contrary, the global economic pie is expanding, and that's good news for all of us. Emerging markets, represented mostly by the countries located in Asia, account for more than 40% of global economic output. (By comparison, the US represents 24% of global GDP.) These countries are home to two-thirds of the world's population and more than three-quarters of its millennials. They have less debt than their more developed counterparts, including the US citizens, and they're contributing to a global population boom that is expected to add 2.5 billion more citizens to the planet over the next 30 years. That means there will be many more people striving to contribute to their societies, to share their talents, and many more people with wants and needs of their own, which will be met in the form of goods and services. There will be many more problems ahead, which means there will be many opportunities to solve them. Investing in publicly traded assets offers each one of us a way to participate in—and profit from—the amazing system that's going to continue driving human progress.

Don't get the wrong idea. I'm not saying that global Capitalism lifts everyone to the same extent, at all times, all across the world. There are eight billion of us, after all, and we're dealing with a lot of variables. Capitalism flourishes in times of peace and harmony, less so in times of conflict and war. It does the most for people in democratic societies, not in dictatorships or oligarchies. Regulation can guide it or work against it, inhibiting the flow of resources where they are most needed. And it certainly doesn't work in a linear fashion. It must constantly correct course for geographic and economic imbalances. But Capitalism is like water—it keeps flowing, finding new routes and passages as others get blocked or dry up. That's why, even after dips and false starts, the global, long-term trend is one of longer lifespans and better standards of living for our species.

We all participate in global Capitalism, but we have the choice to foster a deeper and more rewarding relationship with this system that lifts us closer to our unique personal goals and honors our place as participants in something bigger than ourselves. You can approach investing not as a zero-sum game, but as a tool to help you experience life in the way you most want to experience it and as a force to bring society together and realize accomplishments that no individual could achieve on their own. Internalizing these truths will empower you as an investor and help you become a more well-rounded human being.

That said, I'm well aware that it's not easy to develop this relationship with investing. So much is working against you, from cultural and societal expectations to the machinations of financial professionals working at investment firms, insurance companies, and banks. We use the term "Wall Street" as a collective name for the investment industry, but you're just as susceptible to the practices of "Insurance Street" and "Bank Street"—so I call the group "Financial Street" for short.

Beyond these outside forces, though, the most difficult obstacle to overcome may be your own mind. Taking a close look at the patterns of thought and feeling that have been etched into your conscious and subconscious mind reveals just how large a challenge we all face. But confronting this legacy also puts us in a better position to create new patterns—ones that help us embrace the true power of investing and all that it can bring.

CHAPTER 1 LUMINOUS INSIGHTS

Knowledge is power. To be a successful investor, you must have confidence and faith in where you are investing your surplus savings. Spend time understanding the potential risks and rewards from investing in private relationships to publicly traded securities. You can do this through your own research of financial literary works or spending time with a licensed investment professional with whom you work to help you understand how capital markets work. Don't just turn your money over to even the highest-esteemed professional or institution without having them illustrate in detail their process for managing your valuable assets. There will inevitably be temporary periods when your investments will experience a *decline* in valuation. And you need to understand the resilient properties embedded in the capital markets system and the time needed to propel your investments on a lifetime uptrend. Global Capitalism works. Otherwise, it wouldn't exist!

CONTEMPLATIONS

- What is your belief or knowing about Capitalism?
- To what extent do you trust this system as a way of investing your surplus savings for your future retirement income needs?
- To what extent can you accept that *volatility* is a primary characteristic of participating in this system?
- Take the answers to these questions into conversations with your advisory team.

CHAPTER 2

THE FIRST OBSTACLE: OUR MIND'S PROGRAMMING

Until you make the unconscious conscious, it will direct your life
and you will call it fate.
—CARL JUNG

PICTURE A TYPICAL TWENTY-FIRST-CENTURY INVESTOR: They are at home in front of their computer, sipping a cappuccino they made that morning with their sleek countertop espresso machine, clicking through a series of charts that display their portfolio's performance alongside real-time price updates from the global stock markets. They're studying how their investments have fared over the past day, week, month, year, or decade. They can break down their portfolio by sectors and drill down into specific stocks. They're plugged into an invisible network connecting them to billions of other people and organizations around the world. With access to a staggering amount of information, they believe they have the knowledge and power to be smarter and faster than the other investors they're competing against. They can compare their portfolio to any number of indexes or to hypothetical portfolios—and then use all these data points to decide whether to buy or sell, to change direction or stay the course.

Everything about this scene suggests a highly evolved human making rational, data-driven decisions. Yet beneath these modern trappings, at the level of thought and emotion, this investor is no different from a prehistoric hunter-gatherer sitting in front of a fire, ready to run away from a tiger that jumps out of the bushes or chase after a wayward deer that wanders into their camp.

The environment may have changed over the millennia—instead of watching out for deer and tigers, our investor is ready to chase a hot stock or run away from a market downturn—but the psychology at play is fundamentally the same. Very little about the human brain has changed in the 30,000 or so years since the caveman days. In fact, the structure of our brain is roughly the same as it was when *Homo sapiens* emerged about 350,000 years ago. That's because 350,000 years, while it sounds like a long time, is just a blip in the millions of years of evolution that led up to our emergence as a species. Before humans developed the ability to make tools (or build cities and invest in companies), we were animals living on the savannah, competing for resources with other animals. Our brain reflects that long evolutionary process. Much as we like to imagine otherwise, we're all just cavemen sitting around the fire, alert to any movement in the darkness just beyond our camp.

According to Harvard professor Gerald Zaltman's research, 95% of all cognition takes place in the subconscious mind. We feel that we're in control of our thoughts, but it might be more accurate to say that our thoughts are in control of us. As we go about our day, our brain is buzzing with activity at the subconscious level. It takes in all the information we encounter through our senses and processes it through a complicated network of neural circuits. When it comes time to make a decision or perform an action, that split-second of apparent "control" has been primed by all the stimuli our subconscious mind has been attending to. What we experience as a conscious decision is, in fact, just the final step in a largely subconscious procedure. In effect, our conscious mind is taking orders from our subconscious mind.

You can blame evolution for this situation. Mammal brains evolved from the brains of much less complex creatures. The vestiges of these simpler brains remain with us and form the basis of much of our experience. Think of this primordial cognitive holdover as our lizard brain. Its primary purpose is to control basic bodily functions like breathing, balance, and coordination, as well as simple survival instincts like mating, feeding, and self-defense. Our brain may have evolved to become capable of more complex tasks—we've developed a prefrontal cortex, for example, which helps us make decisions and navigate the social world—but these basic functions have remained in place, controlled by the ancient lizard brain.

One of the oldest parts of our lizard brain is the amygdala, a tiny cluster of neurons that has an outsized effect on our thoughts and emotions. The amygdala helps us process stimuli and sends the appropriate response signals to the rest of our body. If those stimuli seem to pose a threat, it triggers our conscious brain to register fear and take action. All this work happens on a subconscious level, initiating reactions before the more rational parts of our brain have a chance to evaluate the threat. If the lion that jumps out of the bushes turns out to be a housecat, we may already be halfway up a tree before we come to the correct understanding.

This unconscious response is the fight, flight, or freeze instinct that we're all familiar with. It increases our heart rate and respiration and primes us for quick and decisive action. And it's not just physical threats like lions that trigger the amygdala. More abstract threats can have just the same effect.

Let's return to the investor sitting in front of their computer, sipping their homemade cappuccino. Imagine they're looking at their portfolio in late February 2020. They've been reading disturbing news about the coronavirus, and they're getting a little nervous. By the end of the day, the market has taken a significant plunge, and their heart rate has gone the opposite direction—up. They find it hard to turn away from their phone that evening, and they don't sleep well that night. The next day, the market trades down even further. As they sit at their desk looking at the numbers, a drop of sweat forms on the back of their neck. By lunch, they're on their second shirt of the day. If there were a nearby tree, they'd probably climb it. Instead, they dial up their broker, instructing them to sell off stocks—the sooner the better. Their fight-or-flight instinct kicked in, and they flew. Imagine their panic if it's one of those infrequent occasions where the brokerage house phone lines are jammed for the rest of the day.

Over the next month, they watch the markets continue to go down, and a wave of self-congratulation passes over them. They imagine they were pretty smart to get ahead of the markets like they did. They're glad they didn't wait to sell, like so many other investors did.

But their satisfaction starts to dissipate later in the spring as the markets show signs of turning around. You may recall, there was no positive news of any kind hitting the airwaves to indicate a stock market recovery. By summer, the market has fully recovered, and they're cursing themselves for selling out back in February. They think about the gains they've missed out on—not to mention the trading costs and tax consequences of their sell-off. Bad as stocks looked in March 2020 (and not discounting the human toll of the pandemic), their fight-or-flight response failed to serve their best interests.

And yet their reaction aligns with the latest research about how our brain responds to the prospect of losing money. A study by the National Institutes of Health found that the more frequently people were told they were losing money, the more their amygdalas flared up. Meanwhile, a Harvard study showed that even the expectation of financial *losses* triggered frantic activity in the amygdala.

You might think that all it takes to overcome this powerful lizard-brain reaction is to wait for the panic to subside and proceed in a deliberate, rational manner. If only it were this simple. Even as a moment's danger fades into the background of our consciousness, the fight, flight, or freeze reaction has been recorded. Fear reactions etch themselves in our subconscious mind like grooves in a record, and when we encounter new potential dangers, our minds want to fall right back in those grooves. This is one of the many ways our brain is wired to detect patterns—even when the patterns may be illusory.

When our investor saw the dip in their portfolio's performance, their brain didn't just register danger—it subconsciously detected a pattern: this could be the beginning of a larger market slowdown. The thought was bolstered by their memory of the 2008 Great Recession, which they experienced as a traumatic event even though their portfolio quickly recovered from it. For them, as for many investors, every little dip in the market is a sign that the sky might be falling again. And Financial Street and the Media are there to encourage these fears with their own rhetoric.

If just reading about this scenario is making your heart beat faster, here's a quick reality check: since World War II, the US stock market, as measured by the S&P 500 stock index, has experienced

12 bear markets—periods when the price of the index exceeds a 20% decline. The average length of these market downturns is 15.5 months. Every year we experience an average 14% decline from the intra-year peak price. The takeaway—*volatility* is a natural and organic aspect of investing.

The global events that created these temporary periods of panic ranged from the Cuban Missile Crisis to President Kennedy's assassination, to the OPEC oil embargo, to Black Monday's Program Trading Crash, to the Technology Dotcom crash, to the financial and real estate collapse of 2008, to the coronavirus collapse in 2020, and most recently the market declines from the Russian invasion of Ukraine. And through all of the world's wars, civil unrest, economic imbalances, and global tragedies, the S&P 500 index has climbed in price from 58.11 in 1960 to 3,969 in February of 2023. That represents a 10.04% average annual return. A $10,000 lump sum investment would have grown to $4,222,200.

Capitalism and human behavior are messy to witness from day to day. The plumbing system of the capital markets is infinite in its complexity. But it's the best system that exists for the exchange of goods and services, and for rewarding lifetime investors in their participation. Understanding time diversification and the impulse of human decision making is required to be a successful investor. In other words, the sky is not falling today, and it won't fall tomorrow.

The fear, however, is real. And as investors we must recognize and become aware of that fear before it drives us to make bad choices. The most obvious times we succumb to fear are when anxiety about losing money in a downturn makes us sell off our investments. But there's another way that persistent discomfort and anxiety affect our choices. Many of us hold the misconception that investing is just too complicated for all but the most experienced professionals to wrap their minds around. We hear about the array of financial products out there, from annuities to life insurance to mutual funds, hedge funds, real estate, commodities, private equity, and much more, and we recoil at the thought of choosing among them. So, we don't choose.

Some people avoid investing altogether, missing the opportunity to live their dharma. Others simply try to avoid thinking about money and investing as much as possible. About 60% of American workers say that planning for their retirements makes them feel stressed, according to the 2019 Retirement Confidence Survey from the Employee Benefits Research Institute—and it's natural to avoid engaging in activities that cause stress. Rather than face up to the reality of investing (it's not as complicated as the Media or many investing professionals make it out to be), we just follow along blindly with whatever our family, friends, or colleagues are doing, or whatever the Media tells us to do.

This tendency to unconsciously follow whatever other people are doing is called the "herd mentality." You can see it wherever people act mindlessly, going through the motions because it's what their friends, work colleagues, or family are doing. We eat whatever everyone else is eating, travel to the same places everyone travels to, join the same country clubs, and buy the same products everyone buys. Similarly, mindless investors see everyone around them investing in a certain way and simply follow the herd. Everyone raced to buy dot com stocks in the late '90s; real estate seemed like the sure bet in the mid-2000s; more recently it was Google, Facebook, Apple, and Amazon. Following the herd might feel good because you don't have to make an informed decision for yourself, but the herd doesn't always know where it's going. It could be running in circles, for all you know—or worse, heading for a cliff.

Here's an example of the herd effect in action. In 1996, I became the advisor for the employee retirement plan at a large hospital in Greensboro, North Carolina. At that time, it employed well over 5,000 physicians, nurses, and other employees. I had just joined the brokerage arm of a famous national investment company and discovered that this hospital had a retirement plan provided by my firm's insurance division based in New York. Representatives from the New York office only visited the hospital once a year, and I learned that the employees were constantly complaining about the lack of information about their plan and its options. I felt I could do a better job, so I lobbied my bosses to let me take over. I also asked the hospital's HR department to give me an on-site office where I'd work twice a week. Both parties granted my wish.

Soon after taking over the plan and poring over spreadsheets packed with metrics and account information, I discovered something truly odd: about 70% of the plan's total assets were invested in the plan's Guaranteed Interest Account—a type of annuity that pays a very small interest rate and is designed to preserve savings, not provide growth. The rest of the employees' money was split between stocks, bonds, and money market accounts. I'd been around long enough to see my share of people with overly cautious retirement accounts, but I was shocked to discover such a large group of people all investing so conservatively—and in exactly the same way.

To figure out what was going on, I began asking the employees how they chose their investments. To a person, they told me that they'd gone to HR and asked where their coworkers were putting their money. And HR, with their basic knowledge of the plan assets from the annual reviews, told them that their coworkers were putting most of their savings in the Guaranteed Interest Account. It was a self-perpetuating pattern of behavior.

I further discovered that when the plan was introduced decades earlier, the Guaranteed Interest Account was the only investment option available. At that time, in the absence of alternatives, it made sense for employees to invest in those accounts. When I arrived on the scene, there were 17 investment options available—a good mix of annuities, money market funds, bond funds, and stock funds—and it no longer made sense for people to put most of their money in these low-return vehicles. But they continued to exert a gravitational pull, thanks to the herd effect. The hospital's employees simply did what everyone around them was doing.

It was an extreme example, but not totally surprising, since workplace retirement plans are notorious for creating a herd effect. Employees participate in the 401(k) plan because it's what all their co-workers are doing. They all contribute about the same percentage of their checks because that's how much their co-workers are contributing. They're all invested in the same assets because they all got recommendations from the same salesperson at the money management firm in charge of the plan. In fact, the US government is even encouraging this mindless, herd-like behavior by promoting the use of target-date funds as the default "safe harbor" investment for 401(k) plans.

These special funds sound appealing—just pick the fund targeted to the year you want to retire and put all your plan contributions into it. The fund managers are supposed to continually adjust that fund's underlying investment mix to be appropriate for your age—more growth-oriented stocks when you're younger, more "safe" bonds when you're approaching retirement. The trouble is that most of these funds are designed to hold 75% to 80% of your money in bonds when you reach retirement. These portfolios designed for principal protection will systematically erode in value from the 20-plus years of growing spending needs of the retirees due to the ravages of inflation. A far more customized approach is needed to build portfolios for retirees that each have unique life circumstances and desires. The government, mutual fund companies, and employers who offer 401(k) plans have conflicts of interest in these schemes and have conspired to set us up to very slowly, very comfortably run out of money before we die.

An entire body of work in financial literacy has sprung up in recent times attempting to label why people make decisions around aspects of their money. It's referred to as "behavioral economics," and the herd mentality is just one such behavior. It suggests that these behavioral biases and reactions are the cause of our poor results. It follows the universal principles of cause and effect. Change the cause, and change the effect. And if we can simply identify the cause, then we can stop the behavior, and we can positively change the effects of our money results.

This body of work, which is embedded in the financial ecosystem, does not work in practice. It assumes that we can make conscious-level choices using survival-level conditioning of the subconscious mind. While entertaining for the financial institutions and their customers, it is an unrewarding exercise of the intellect.

Because it is so pervasive in its use, I will mention just a few of the behavioral terms you may be presented with. You may be labeled to have a "familiarity bias." This bias indicates that people over-weight their investment holdings with familiar investments. They believe these securities will be either safer or higher returning without commensurate *volatility*, even though clearly, we can't all be correct at once. Those with this bias tend to also be more comfortable than they should be by bulking up on their employer's stock in a retirement plan. You can imagine how employees of the once fifth-largest company in the US stock market felt after their Enron company went bankrupt.

You may be labeled to have a "confirmation bias." Investors love to be right and hate to be wrong. This trait is revealed when we are paying extra attention to information that supports our beliefs and we're especially suspicious of, or even entirely blind to, conflicting evidence. This can be extremely costly. It's obviously important to have the attributes of objectivity when making important decisions about financial assets.

Finally, but far from exhausting the list of behavioral labels, you may be accused of having an "anchoring bias." This occurs when you fixate on a reference point, whether or not it's a valid one. This is helpful if you've given your son or daughter a curfew time of 10 p.m. But investors will fall prey to this bias when they anchor the value of an investment holding by what they paid for it. They may decide, for example, to just hold their position that is underwater until it returns to their original investment value. Certainly not considering adding to their position. Following a professionally written investment policy statement will inform us the best time to buy, hold, or sell holdings based on the portfolio's predetermined asset allocation targets. It is this response system that guides the decisions made in portfolio management, not the reactions of human emotions or fixated myths. It is possible that in this example, rather than taking no action on the holding, there would have been additional purchases made. In rare circumstances, due to a material change in investment fundamentals, a sale would be made irrespective of purchase price, so anchoring on arbitrary price points creates a dangerous distraction.

To avoid the effects of herd mentality means that you must decide what philosophical strategy you want to apply, then choose the investments that serve your personal vision and journey, irrespective of what all others are doing. Just because a million people are heading for a cliff doesn't mean that you should join them. Crafting a well-thought-out master financial plan is tough for a lot of people because most Americans haven't been taught how to save properly, much less how to invest. Financial education just isn't part of our culture. Determining what financial information is important to managing your wealth successfully without stress is foundational. Knowledge, experience, faith, and discernment are key attributes to have.

Remember, though—results stemming from a herd mentality and other labels developed by behavioral economics are a symptom of a bigger condition—not a cause. The cause is the fight, flight, or freeze reactions and tribal conditioning that lie deep in the recesses of the most ancient part of our brain. That's why it's such a pervasive problem and one that financial literacy alone isn't enough to eradicate. What's worse, biological instinct is only one way our subconscious mind works against us. How our minds are formed by outside influences throughout our lives—but especially in our crucial early years—also plays an impactful role in the way we make investment decisions. These environmental factors combine with our evolutionary inheritance to compound the power that our subconscious exerts upon us. Focus on reprogramming your mind (cause), and you will see the positive results (effects). In this next chapter, we will explore our environmental, social, and familial conditioning.

CHAPTER 2 LUMINOUS INSIGHTS

Volatility is a natural and organic aspect of investing in stocks. We must refrain from our fight, flight, or freeze reactions during the expected temporary stock market *declines*, "breaking-news" headlines of the Media, and fears expressed by our co-workers, family, friends, and religious leaders. We must avoid following the herd mentality and develop a custom investment game plan that serves our unique goals. It is time in the market and not market timing that is an investor's friend. It takes knowledge, emotional intelligence, patience, and faith to be a successful investor.

CONTEMPLATIONS

- Your task here is to simply recognize what state of readiness and emotional perspective you are in, in the context of these questions.

- To what extent do you follow the herd with your actions or go right when most everyone else is going left?
- How established is your investment philosophy and game plan?
- How did you decide on your investment choices?
- Are you capable of managing your own portfolio without advice?
- To what degree do you make investment decisions after listening to colleagues, friends, and family?
- Do you follow the advice of a registered investment advisory professional?
- How do you react or respond to investment market fluctuations?
- Do you feel centered and perhaps opportunistic when seeing stock market values drop, or do you feel deeply concerned and perhaps stressed, feeling the need to withdraw?

CHAPTER 3

THE SECOND OBSTACLE: OUR CULTURAL CONDITIONING

Give me the child until he is seven and I'll give you the man.
—ARISTOTLE

DEEP IN THE SIERRA NEVADA de Santa Marta Mountain range in northern Colombia lives an indigenous group called the Kogi. The Kogi are descendants of a highly advanced culture that pre-dates the arrival of European settlers in South America. The isolation of their mountain villages has kept them more or less free from the influence of modern civilization.

For guidance and healing, the Kogi turn to a class of spiritual leaders called Mamos. In Kogi culture, not just anyone can become a Mamo. A select few male children are chosen at birth to enter this elite group, and their training begins immediately. For Mamos, training doesn't entail years of scholarship as it would for a priest in modern society. Instead, Mamos spend the first nine years of their life in a dark cave, where elder Mamos, along with the child's mother, care for him and teach him how to tune in to Aluna, or the "Great Mother," the creative force that the Kogi believe flows through the universe.

In a culture already cut off from the rest of the world geographically, Mamos are further isolated from the rest of Kogi society. They eat, sleep, and devote hours upon hours meditating in order to cultivate their connection to the life force that animates all beings. When they finally emerge from their caves after nine years, they spend the rest of their lives leading their people in religious ceremonies and serving as a resource for questions about the nature of existence.

For those of us living in post-industrial Western society, nine years in a cave sounds incredibly drastic. But modern science suggests that the Kogi may be on to something. The first seven or so years of our lives have been shown to play a determinative role in the formation of our subconscious minds. It's during these years that we learn how to think and act in the world by observing and absorbing the examples from people all around us. In effect, we're learning how to become members of our tribes—our family, our society, and our culture.

But it's not as if we're consciously studying and taking notes on the correct way to live. Instead, the way to live is downloaded directly into our subconscious mind. We accept all the information from our environment as a given that's difficult to challenge or change. This information includes attitudes about money, work, self-worth, relationships, religion, material possessions, lifestyle, and the rules for how the global community operates. When we step back and examine our lives, however, we can see that the way we internalize the attitudes and emotions of our culture constitutes a kind of hypnosis. And this hypnosis, left unchecked, can last your entire life.

Learning to embrace a wealth management approach that offers a more peaceful, meaningful, and happy life involves de-hypnotizing yourself—freeing yourself from the unconscious programming you absorbed as a child. It requires you to shed the layers of environmental influence that encoded desires and inclinations in your mind—desires that may or may not reflect your most authentic self. It involves facing up to fears that have no basis in objective reality. It means tapping into the deepest part of yourself and asking yourself what you truly want. It's too late to go back and spend the first nine years of your life in a cave, but with conscious awareness, intention, and consistent effort we can all learn to recognize and reprogram our subconscious conditioning.

Let's take a closer look at this conditioning. Our parents— along with other influential family members and friends—are among the most important environmental influences that shape our young minds. In fact, our parents' influence starts even before we're born. The genetic material of our mother and father—itself formed from the genetic material of their parents, grandparents, great-grandparents, and so on—determines not only our physical makeup, but much of our mental and emotional makeup as well.

Likewise, the time we spend in our mother's womb shapes us in many ways. For these nine months, our mother is our whole world. The emotional stresses and fears a mother experiences during these months (as well as the moments of peace and joy) are literally felt and absorbed by the being developing inside her. The environmental substances she consumes—the nutritional value of diet (healthy or unhealthy) and effects of medications, for example—are passed directly to the child. Many of the anxieties we experience later in life, including financial anxieties, can be traced back to these earliest moments of our existence.

Once we're born, of course, the influence of our family manifests in a thousand different ways. How many young people end up working jobs they have no passion for simply because it's what their parents expected of them? When we're children, our minds are sponges, soaking up everything in our environment. Developmentally, our young minds are operating at an alpha, theta, and delta level of frequency. We don't have the capacity yet to challenge the information that's constantly streaming into us. We can't say, "No, that's not who I am" or "I don't think that's true." This unquestioning receptiveness makes us perfect receptacles for our parents' fears and desires. When we consider that our parents' minds were perfect receptacles for the fears and desires of their parents—and so on down the generational line—it's easy to see that our world is full of people trying to live the lives of all the people who came before them, the unacknowledged creators of their subconscious programming. Our minds become the garbage bins for everyone else's histories.

Sometimes, the parental influence on a person's attitude toward money can be glaringly obvious. Early in my career, I took on a client who told me in one of our quarterly meetings that he had no interest in the stock market. All but a small percentage of his portfolio was in municipal bonds. This guy was the COO of a large, publicly traded fast food company, so I was more than a little surprised by his admission. When I asked him to share more about his perspective, he told me that many decades ago his father had invested heavily in a railroad stock, to the exclusion of all other

25

investment opportunities. The company had gone bankrupt, and as a result his father had sworn off stocks altogether.

My client's entire attitude toward investing had been formed by his father's reaction to an isolated market event. Never mind that my client's extremely diversified portfolio of global companies was performing quite well. Never mind that if his father had invested in a broader array of securities, his portfolio would have been able to easily absorb the shock of the railroad company's bankruptcy. This client had unconsciously learned to fear owning stocks by witnessing his father's ill-advised attempt to save his surplus earnings in a single security (which is known as "unsystematic risk" in the financial world). He let it control his behavior. And the fear was so strong that it crowded out all other emotions and ideas about investing.

Other family influences are more subtle. I've seen people whose reckless attitude toward money is a sort of rebellion against their parents' frugality. Or someone's extreme anxiety around money might stem from a family member who blew their savings. Or maybe your family never talked about money—that's something I see in clients all the time. You're left to soak up what lessons you can, and often they're not the most helpful ones. Discovering the full extent of family influences is a lengthy process, and I'll talk more about what it involves—and why it's necessary—in Chapter 5. For now, it's enough to identify family as a major contributor toward unconscious investing.

Take another step back, and we can see that our family is merely one node in a vast complex of systems that together form our subconscious attitudes and beliefs. Broader societal and cultural influences also make their mark on us as soon as we come into the wider community. In school, we're taught to value certain kinds of behavior and not others. Advertising seduces our minds to chase after certain material objects that we otherwise might not want. The government dictates our attitudes in many areas of life, from how we should be eating, what kind of medical care we should have, to how we should think about retirement. For some people, religion is a powerful influence.

When it comes to money and investing, the combined influence of our family, the Media, our friends and colleagues, the government, and other outside forces acts on us in ways that are so powerful it can be hard to see them operating. You end up experiencing life from the perspective of how you were programmed. Your beliefs become your reality.

These forces form a collective unconscious in our society and determine many of the decisions we make as individuals. If "collective unconscious" seems a little out there to you, maybe you'll be comfortable with the term "conventional wisdom." Think about the investing ideas that have been passed down through our culture from generation to generation and that go more or less unchallenged by most people. Here's one example: "Buy more bonds as you near retirement." Even if you can't remember a specific time you heard this advice, you've probably absorbed it from the cultural ether. And, on the face of it, it makes sense. When you're younger, goes the story, you can afford to accept more *volatility*. You might as well put most of your investments in stocks, knowing that you have plenty of time to recover from cyclically common market downturns. When you're older and no longer bringing in a regular salary, you're better off moving that money into bonds, which are in the short term lower in volatility. Stocks are too risky to depend on in retirement, or so we've been conditioned to believe. But this is another case in which the stories our culture tells itself are obscuring reality.

I've had clients who've gone their entire lives investing mostly in stocks. They have more money than they need to fulfill all their hopes and dreams, and we've developed a lifetime, equity-based plan that would allow them to live the lifestyle they want even if another Great Depression hit. I've run all the models and shown them the projections. I've used three different evidence-based financial appraisal methodologies to show them that they will never run out of money before they die. There's no reason to change course. Then one day, usually when they're 63 or 64, something inside them shifts, and they come to me and say, "I guess we'll be getting more into bonds." They're not particularly excited about the idea, but to them it seems inevitable. It's like the decision has been made for them. We're all so conditioned to believe certain "truths" about investing that it never occurs to us to challenge them. "Buy more bonds as you near retirement," like so many other nuggets of conventional wisdom, has been baked into our society's financial DNA.

The impact of cultural conditioning is so deep-rooted and powerful that it sets in motion patterns of thought and behavior. From childhood on, our subconscious conditioning expresses itself in certain tendencies—to be healthy or unhealthy, extroverted or introverted, optimistic or pessimistic, emotionally centered or emotionally turbulent, overachieving or self-sabotaging, and so on. A major trauma event (e.g., a family altercation) can translate into a mood, which over time translates into a temperament, which further becomes one's personality if left unchecked. Like the fear responses that store themselves in our memory bank, the tendencies we express again and again become grooves in the record of our subconscious mind. Those grooves translate into habits that guide our actions with little or no conscious direction.

Good habits help us achieve the goals we form in our conscious mind, but bad coding in our subconscious programming can keep us from reaching those goals—no matter how much we think we want them. Our unconscious mind sabotages our conscious desires. Some bad habits express themselves as voices inside our heads, telling us that we can't do something hard, that it can wait until tomorrow, or that we don't deserve the success we so strongly desire.

Before I entered the world of financial advising, my passion was golf. I began playing at the age of five and received formal instructions at the age of 12. My mentor, Banks Guyton, an accomplished playing professional in his own right, etched into my psyche to be the best that I could be, no matter my career path. I had great success with the game of golf, attending the University of South Carolina on scholarship and being given the honor of team captain my final two years. It taught me so many of life's treasured lessons. I had much early success as an amateur and played at a high level in national amateur events before turning pro. I played with many golfers in college and on the national amateur circuit who had the résumés and physical talent to be PGA Tour players, but they didn't reach that stage because they listened to an inner voice that kept telling them they didn't deserve it. Other players had less innate skill or more unconventional swings, but they made the Tour because their inner voices told them they were professional golfers. Those voices gave them self-confidence and allowed them to feel at ease on a big stage. It was their positive subconscious programming from their early years of life that supported their conscious desires. So much of life comes down to confidence or the lack of it.

One summer when I was a teenager, I had five big golf tournaments coming up over a three-week span. I remember standing in front of my mirror one morning, thinking about the tournaments coming up and knowing deep within my being that I was going to win all five. I could see myself being focused, hitting the shots I needed to hit, sinking the putts, hoisting the trophies, and the emotions that followed. I was living the results in the present moment.

And believe it or not, I went on to win those five tournaments. That's when I first began to truly understand that I was more than just my physical body. There's an aspect of ourselves beyond our physical body and five senses. Over years of practice, I'd built up the confidence necessary to imagine being highly competitive on the national amateur stage. My subconscious programming installed in my early years of development supported my conscious desires with my golfing achievements. The lesson I took from witnessing not only my experience but that of many other talented golfing comrades is this—you get who you are, not what you want.

Over the course of my career, I've observed that many people have been programmed to feel that they don't deserve wealth and well-being. Their inner voices tell them they'll never be able to afford the vacation home on Martha's Vineyard, they can't find a way to take a year sabbatical from their career to travel the world, they don't have what it takes to leave their unsatisfying job to start a business reflecting their passions, or they can't see a way to impact their charitable interests. There are challenges to reaching these goals, of course, but everyone is capable of overcoming hurdles and achieving their passionate desires. We only think we can't because we give too much credit to our inner voices, telling us we're not capable enough. Our mind's programming says you aren't worthy, when in reality you are. It may take some time to get rid of your bad habits and build up a sense of yourself that's strong enough to manifest your desires, but it can be done.

Bad habits can manifest in any and all areas of your life, from your career choice and your choice of partner to the things you buy and how you spend your free time. We think we make these choices in full awareness, using logic and reason to chart out the path that best fits our long-term desires. In reality, our subconscious mind controls so many of these choices—the same subconscious mind that's been fed all sorts of signals over the years from the culture in which we live. We see our neighbors buying bigger houses, driving fancier cars, and taking exotic vacations, and we feel compelled to follow the same path.

Sometimes we make decisions that seem wise at the time but gradually become ill-suited to us as our life and needs evolve. We launch a career we're excited about only to find it's no longer fulfilling ten years down the line. Or we make big purchases that go unused after an initial period of enthusiasm. Yet habit and subconscious conditioning keep us trapped by those decisions, and our inability to move on becomes just another pattern in our minds—a groove on the record that the needle keeps replaying over and over. When we're stuck like this, we need to pause and remind ourselves of our highest and deepest need—to live our dharma and enjoy a life that's authentically our own.

Here's an example of how that can happen. A few years ago, I met with a couple that was distraught about their finances and confused about the direction their lives were taking. Michael was a surgeon, and his wife, Susan, managed a vineyard she'd inherited from her parents and grandparents. They were approaching retirement and arrived for their first meeting with me visibly distressed. Michael was making over $900,000 a year, but his career had become a source of intense stress. He and two partners owned a $5-million building and were struggling to pay the mortgage. They'd bought the building at the peak of the real estate boom. The economic crisis of 2008 caused them to lose a lot of tenants, which put pressure on their cash flow. Now their mortgage was higher than the value of the building, and nine months after they'd put it on the market, it had failed to sell. On top of that, Michael was consistently a lot more productive than his partners but receiving equal pay.

Meanwhile, Susan's vineyard wasn't bringing in the revenues it had in its heyday when her parents and grandparents owned it. Susan felt a sense of responsibility to keep the vineyard in the family, but she had no passion for the day-to-day work of running it. Like Michael, she came from a well-to-do family and felt a lot of pressure to follow in their footsteps. One way that manifested in their lives was in having a million-dollar mortgage on a small yacht, a marker of their success and their status as high achievers.

I saw that Michael and Susan were hanging on to things because they had always had them. Michael's medical practice was in disarray. His yacht no longer brought him pleasure. Susan's vineyard was being neglected in favor of other interests. They'd lost sight of who they truly were. After updating their balance sheet and talking through budget issues, I asked the couple this question, "What brings you joy?"

It's a simple question, but it requires profound reflection. Michael and Susan had a hard time answering it. They both pondered a bit, looked at each other, and came up completely empty. They left my office—they were heading to a medical conference in Boca Raton, Florida—and we planned to reconvene a few weeks later.

When Michael and Susan came into our next meeting, I knew something had changed—they both looked like they were walking two feet off the ground. They sat down, and Michael told me he'd had a revelation. "You asked what brought us joy," he said. "I didn't have an answer at that moment, but while we were away, it became self-evident. She's sitting right next to me. It doesn't matter what we have or don't have, as long as I have Susan. Oh, and by the way, I've already found a buyer for the yacht."

My heart was smiling. Asking Michael and Susan to reflect on their true desires—"What brings you joy?"—had helped them to break out of a pattern that no longer served them, and from that decision to sell the yacht came a cascade of positive, habit-breaking developments. My colleagues and I worked with Michael to find a buyer for his building. His partners were able to continue their practice there, and Michael was able to retire. Meanwhile, Susan sold her vineyard and became an ayurvedic practitioner with a practice attached to their beautifully wooded residential property.

After a while, they discovered that they missed being out on the water, but they didn't want the burden of owning a yacht, so they joined a boat club on a lake near where they lived. For a very reasonable monthly fee, they could choose from a variety of boats available to use any day they wanted without any of the trappings of ownership. They just had to call the club in advance and ask to have their boat ready and waiting for their arrival. When they finished for the day, they simply returned the boat to the dock. No trailers, no insurance, no repairs, no cleaning up—just the simple pleasure of doing something together, something that brought them joy.

Michael and Susan's story illustrates the power of breaking out of unhelpful patterns of thought and behavior. It shows that problems are solved on a different level of consciousness than that on which they were created. Once they looked inside for their inner peace, their outer world began to reflect back to them their renewed light. They became luminous.

Like so many stories I've witnessed in my years as an advisor, their story demonstrates the ways in which our lives can flourish when we become conscious of the ways our minds have been programmed. Your subconscious mind, shaped by evolution, family influences, and cultural conditioning, can in fact be harnessed to serve your deepest needs and desires. And it was that simple question—"What brings you joy?"—that allowed them to hit the pause button on their life and ultimately switch gears. You can hit that pause button, too.

But before we move on, we must confront one more obstacle that stands between you and your ability to live your dharma—our financial institutions. The major players in the industry that we rely on to build financial security and wealth cannot always be trusted to act in your best interests. Far too many financial professionals actually exploit their clients for their own gain—and they do this by virtue of understanding your subconscious mind better than you do. This is the subject of the next chapter.

CHAPTER 3 LUMINOUS INSIGHTS

Learning to embrace a wealth management approach that offers a more peaceful, meaningful, and happy life involves de-hypnotizing yourself—freeing yourself from the unconscious programming you absorbed as a child. We need to rewire our subconscious mind to match the desires of our authentic conscious world. For most people, we only wake up to needed changes of our behavioral patterns when bad things happen—broken marriages, lost jobs, heart attacks, DUIs, mental depression, etc. And not even then, are we guaranteed to make the course corrections. That's how powerful the subconscious mind is. But we don't have to wait for the bad event to awaken to our highest potential. To live our dharma. Problems are never solved on the same level of consciousness that creates them. You have to work on your inner peace. Change the perspective you have been living with, change who you are, and you change the world. As we saw with Michael and Susan, focusing on who they were, manifested a far different outer world—one that was luminous.

CONTEMPLATIONS

- To what degree do you look at the world with pessimism or optimism?
- Do you feel at times you are a victim of your circumstances or a choice-maker and director of your life?
- To what extent do you trust that life supports your passionate desires, or do you see forces working against your efforts?
- Do you feel that we are all separate beings with five senses doing the best we can with our physical efforts and intelligence, or do you feel there is a non-physical aspect of yourself connected to a higher power guiding your every thought and feeling?
- These are just a few of the perspectives that were formed in your early subconscious programming. If you can determine what is not serving your highest good and label it, you have the opportunity to change it.
- What in your outer world is not serving you? You can change that.
- Most of us—at some level—have participated in writing down our "to do" list for life and maybe have created vision boards for what we want "to have." To prepare yourself for change, your shift in consciousness, begin by writing down your "to be" list.

CHAPTER 4

THE THIRD OBSTACLE: WALL STREET, BANK STREET, AND INSURANCE STREET

*Corruption exists within those that are already corrupt. Power,
or the illusion of it, simply gives already corrupt individuals the
opportunity to express their corruption. In a society where self-
awareness is the norm, corruption is irrelevant. In a society where
there is little or no self-awareness, corruption is a serious problem.*
—*THE ART OF PEACE* BY MORIHEI UESHIBA AND JOHN
STEVENS

A FEW YEARS AGO, A CLIENT of mine asked me to review his father's portfolio. The father was starting to get up there in years—he had recently turned 80—and had moved in with his son. His wife had passed a few years earlier, but he was still capable of caring for himself, and my client was welcoming of his new houseguest. Now that he was around him more, however, he did notice that his father's memory and attention to detail were slipping. My client was in a position that's increasingly common: caring for aging parents who had once cared for us.

The father had been working with a Miami investment broker for many years and had done pretty well for himself, having lived beneath his means and saved systematically since he started his very first job. By investing in a moderate, growth-oriented portfolio of stocks and bonds, he'd accumulated about a million dollars. A few years earlier, he had been living quite comfortably on social security, a pension income, and the dividend and interest income from his investment portfolio that helped him weather temporary stock price declines. He didn't need to sell the principal of his stock and bond holdings to supplement those sources.

But as I reviewed his financial records, I saw something strange: just over a year earlier, he'd sold all his stocks and bonds with substantial gains and put his money into a variable annuity—an insurance product that can provide guarantees of income, growth, and a minimum death benefit depending on the client's needs (and the persuasiveness of an investment broker's sales pitch). Later, I learned his long-time broker had convinced him to make this move.

I could practically hear the broker's pitch: "You don't know how many years you have left. Stocks and bonds are great when you're building savings, but now that you're about to turn 80, don't you want to protect what you have? Don't you want to leave something for your son and daughter? If you let me manage your assets with these guaranteed riders that this annuity offers, you can have the upside potential of the stock markets without the downside risk of their price declines." Who doesn't want to protect what they have and leave something for their kids? How could my client's father say no? He could have all he had before and more. What an offer!

The problem was it was just a story, and that story served one purpose: ensuring the broker's self-interest. Why was this broker suddenly so concerned about protecting his aging client's savings? It turned out that age 80 was the cut-off age for purchasing a variable annuity from this insurance company.

The stock portfolio he sold to purchase the annuity had achieved substantial gains, so he had to pay big capital gains taxes to Uncle Sam before funneling the remaining proceeds into the annuity—taxes he would have avoided had he held the portfolio intact until eventually passing it down to the next generation.

Worse, the broker almost certainly didn't highlight a crucial fact when he sold the annuity: he (the broker) would be collecting an 8% commission. For my client's father, that 8% translated to $80,000. This type of commission is a required disclosure, but it's typically buried in tiny print in an 89-page prospectus, and it doesn't show up on the statement of an investor's new account.

The insurance companies are allowed to illustrate the full value of a customer's investment as if the transaction had no commission. Meanwhile, this new "protective" strategy was charging exorbitant annual fees: 1.25% for the insurance company's mortality and expense feature, 1.10% for the investment funds, and another 1.75% for other rider guarantees. What this meant is that under the guise of protecting his savings, the client was diverting money away from his inheritors and into the pockets of the insurance company and broker.

What about the broker's pitch about leaving something for his family? Annuities are among the worst tax bombs for inheritors: if the investments in the annuity had outperformed the high fees, the next generation would have to pay ordinary income tax on the earnings at the time of withdrawal. Had the original portfolio been left intact, the securities would have received a step up in tax cost basis; thus, the children would owe no taxes when selling them.

In the end, the broker used the power of storytelling to prey on my client's father's inability to understand the complex and opaque insurance world. When I heard my client's father speak about his relationship with his broker, I could tell there was an intimidation factor at play. On top of that, the length of time that he had worked with this gentleman overrode the impulse to question his sales pitch.

Clearly, this broker didn't have his client's best interests in mind. Time was running out. He saw an opportunity to make a sale, and he made it. Because at the end of the day, that's what he was—a salesman. What's more, he made the sale by taking advantage of his client's fears about running out of money and not being able to provide for his loved ones. These fears were likely lodged in the client's subconscious and no doubt reinforced by decades of negative messaging from his immediate environment and our culture at large. The broker knew he could exploit these fears, and he did.

I've been in the business long enough to know that this broker wasn't just a bad apple. The ugly truth is that the majority of representatives posing as financial professionals are just salespeople. Their job is to use your money to meet the sales quotas mandated by their employers and to make money for themselves. That's what they've been trained to do, and that's how the wheels of Financial

Street turn. If you, the client, make money too, that's okay—but it's not their priority. In this particular food chain, you are third in line. I talked earlier about the power of Capitalism to bring people together to do great things. What happens on Financial Street, all too often, is the corruption of this power. The effect is to divide people by pitting firm against firm, advisor against advisor, and— most troublingly—regular investors against each other.

Here's a crucial distinction: Financial Street and Capitalism are not the same thing. Think of Financial Street as an ugly outgrowth of Capitalism. Capitalism harnesses the creative power of millions of people all around the world, culminating in companies that enhance our lives and that we can partially own by becoming investors. When I say "Financial Street," I mean the institutions and individuals that piggyback on these companies to sell investment products to investors. Their goal is to benefit themselves, not the people who buy products from them. They are unnecessary intermediaries, middlemen.

To understand how we got here, consider where we came from. We take it for granted that everyone is now an investor, or at least has the opportunity to be one. We also have countless financial products to choose from. But it hasn't always been this way. In fact, the financial services industry as we know it today is a relatively recent phenomenon.

Investing has been around for centuries, but it wasn't originally a system for the vast majority of us to save for our life's goals. Stock investing originated to help launch companies and fund major public projects. In the early 17th century, the Dutch East India Company became the first company to issue bonds and stock shares to the general public to help finance its fleet of ships. For the first time in history, investors were pooling their money to pay for big commercial ventures, helping to fuel the trade of spices and luxury goods between Europe and Asia.

Similarly, the first American corporations were chartered in the 19th century to perform specific public functions like digging canals and building railroads. In this way, public investment drove the Industrial Revolution and helped elevate America to the status of a global economic superpower. For a long time, however, the number of people with the means and knowledge to invest remained relatively small. Unlike today, there was no expectation that ordinary people with average incomes would take part-ownership of enormous companies. Farmers and shop-owners went about their daily work while a handful of business leaders and speculators invested as part of their professional lives.

Remember, also, that in those days, ordinary people didn't need to invest to help pay for late-in-life expenses. Life expectancies generally were much shorter than they are today. Many people could work until the day they died, and retirements, for the people who could afford them, were short. The concept of collecting income from invested assets in one's retirement years would have been foreign to most people. Even as late as the mid-20th century, many workers were looking at retirements of five to ten years. My father, who worked for the Amoco oil refinery in Yorktown, Virginia, for 30 years, saw his colleagues retiring at 65 and passing away at 70 or 72. He retired at 59 1/2, hoping to enjoy at least a decade of retirement. He ended up living another 31 years, during which time I became his advisor, and he invested heavily in the global stock market. He led a rich and full third act of his life, becoming a farmer and golfing regularly. And, by the way, he never owned a bond!

My father's story is indicative of a change that happened in the middle of the 20th century. Modern medicine, financial prosperity through the worldwide trading of goods and services, and public health advancements significantly boosted life expectancies. Meanwhile, the corporations that had blossomed with the help of Financial Street investors began to employ a larger proportion of American workers. These employees expected longer retirements than those of previous generations and could no longer rely on savings to cover late-in-life expenses. Corporations understood this reality and began offering retirement packages known as "pensions," which provided a lifetime stipend for workers after they retired. But while pensions brought the benefits of investing to ordinary people for the first time in human history, workers remained a step removed from the actual investment process. A small group of professionals with a specialized skill set managed pension assets on behalf of workers, which meant there was no direct relationship between the financial industry and most average Americans.

Compare that scenario with what's happened over the past 40-plus years since the advent of the 401(k) plan. Companies that once managed pensions for their workers have handed off that responsibility to employees themselves. In theory, this change empowers ordinary workers, giving them unprecedented control of their investments and, by extension, their post-work years. In practice, though, most workers have little interest in selecting a mix of assets and have virtually no training to effectively manage a multi-decade investment strategy, nor the emotional fortitude needed to weather volatile periods. Additionally, employers have largely neglected their fiduciary responsibility with disorganized and expensive investment management offerings. For employers, it's a way to reduce costs and transfer the liability of managing other people's money.

In short, we've all been thrown into a system that wasn't originally designed for us, creating an immense gap between the potential of our investments to improve our lives and our ability to harness that potential.

Into this gap has stepped an army of salespeople presenting themselves as financial professionals. In this country, and around the world, managing money is big business—and getting bigger. In 1947, the financial services industry represented 2.35% of the US GDP. By 2018, that figure had tripled to 7.4%. This industry includes stock traders and financial advisors, but it also includes a much broader network of financial personnel working for banks, insurance companies, real estate companies, accounting firms, and law firms. Our participation in the national and international economy is mediated by a priest-like class of specialists who hold the keys to the financial kingdom—or at least we imagine they do. So, we turn to these experts expecting them to look out for our best interests. In entrusting these people with our money, we entrust them with a part of our lives. In reality, though, we're at the bottom of the hierarchy, and the people at the top aren't looking after us.

Here's the equation to understand: the profits at a Financial Street firm aren't driven by the gains they achieve from making sensible investments. Instead, they are largely driven by the fees and commissions they generate by moving someone's savings from one investment product to another. Money in motion drives

Financial Street's profits. That's why financial representatives put so much time and energy into the stories of selling various investment products.

> *Simplicity is a great virtue, but it requires hard work to achieve*
> *it and education to appreciate it. And to make matters worse:*
> *complexity sells better!*
> —EDSGER W. DIJKSTRA, DUTCH COMPUTER SCIENTIST
> AND PROFESSOR EMERITUS, 1999 UT

Like any good salesperson, Financial Street knows why you make the decisions you make. They understand your mind better than you do. They know that it's your reactive reptilian brain that drives so much of your decision making, and they target that part of your brain with the most effective tools available: stories, myths, language, and even dramatic sound effects.

Human beings are natural storytellers. Thousands of years ago, stories were the means by which information was handed down from generation to generation. Stories of how to hunt different animals, where to find the nearest water source, how to heal the body, how to grow food, how to fight in battle—these all served the purpose of keeping us alive and defending us against outside threats. We're wired to react with unquestioning obedience to stories—it's in our DNA—and we love to listen to them. Unfortunately, that means that stories can also be used against us, and that's exactly what the salespeople of Financial Street have mastered. The stories the broker fed my client's father (that I talked about at the beginning of this chapter) are a perfect example. Financial Street tells elaborate and convincing stories about investment opportunities, insurance products, and financial strategies, not for the wealth benefit of the listening audience but for the profit motive of the storyteller.

The Media is a frequent collaborator with Financial Street, and they have even more tools at their disposal when it comes to telling stories that compel investors to react against their best interests. If you listen to Bloomberg or MSNBC pundits describe a stock price decline, you can hear the alarm in the inflections of their voices, often augmented by foreboding music. Conversely, when they talk about positive economic news, their voices and movements are soft and calm. But you don't hear that as often as the negative rhetoric. Conflict makes for better stories, after all, and stories are what hold viewers' attention.

Myths are a special kind of story that circulates throughout a particular culture. They're often created to explain broad rules of thumb of how the world should work or to establish a shared cultural identity. While some myths may have some basis in historical fact, they are often symbolic and should not be taken as literal truth. Financial Street loves myths because they can help reinforce the overarching narrative that you need to keep your money in constant motion.

Here's one example of a Financial Street myth: when you retire at 65 (and not a year earlier), you should have 65% of your money in bonds and you should increase this weighting by 1% with each passing year. This simply isn't true—a higher stock-to-bond ratio will be more beneficial for everyone—but if enough people believe the myth, it will keep Financial Street busy and keep them lining their pockets with completely unnecessary fees and commissions. With this strategy, most investors will slowly run out of purchasing power and money before they die.

The language Financial Street uses when it tells its stories isn't arbitrary. In fact, it's very specific and purposeful. Think about how often you hear the word "*loss*" from so-called financial professionals and their Media cronies. Almost always, what they're talking about is a "*decline,*" not a *loss*. For a *decline* to become a *loss*, you have to sell your investment. Without a sale, there is no *loss*, just a *decline*, which is temporary. But Financial Street knows that you place three times as much emotional weight on price *declines* as you do on price increases of the same magnitude, so they use the scarier, more extreme word—*loss*—to encourage you to sell a certain stock or switch to a different financial product. Using the word "*loss,*" in other words, drives people who should be experiencing temporary *declines* to experience actual *losses*.

Another example: Financial Street loves the word "*risk*." Most often, what they're really talking about is "*volatility,*" not risk. Owning one or two stocks is risky, it's true. You're in trouble if something goes wrong with those individual companies. But owning shares in 10,000 companies around the globe is not risky. There will be some *volatility* in the portfolio because there will be some winners and some losers in the mix. There will be temporary economic downturns. But thanks to the ever-churning growth engine of Capitalism, the winners always outnumber the losers. And the human qualities and attributes of solving problems and imbalances in the capital system carries global economic expansion ever higher after these short-term *declines*. Lifetime investors don't face risk, they accept a certain amount of *volatility*. "*Risk*" is a stronger word, though, because it communicates fear directly with your reptilian brain, so it's the word that Financial Street has standardized and that we've come to accept. Language and storytelling are tools financial agents and brokers use to capture our imaginations. What about the packaging they use to capture our money? Look no further than the array of fees they charge; fees for particular products (like annuities and life insurance), commissions (or bid-ask spreads) on every stock and bond trade, fees charged on the money you put into mutual funds, entry fees and performance-based fees on hedge funds, margin fees when leveraging your portfolio, fees charged on the money you take out of funds. There are fees for providing custody for your retirement accounts, for closing accounts, and for transferring accounts from one institution to another. Additionally, it's not uncommon for major investment brokerage houses to require that clients leave 3% in cash deposits uninvested in stock, bond, or real estate funds. That's another way they make their money.

The same goes for banks. When you deposit money in your account, the bank's priority is not to provide you an interest rate that rewards you for saving. Instead, they use this money as the inventory to make car loans, margin loans, personal loans, credit card offerings, mortgages, HELOCs, and other products that generate revenues for the bank. You can be sure they'll charge the highest rate the market will bear on these offerings while paying you next to nothing on your deposits. That way, they make more profit. And these are just some of the costs you might face when trying to invest your savings.

Insurance companies charge a huge array of commissions on their life insurance, disability income, and long-term care policies that are never discussed with the consumer. Are you aware that a life insurance broker may make as much as 125% of your annual premium in the form of an upfront commission? And then receive hefty ongoing renewal commissions for years to come?

On too many occasions, I've had new clients reveal a prior purchase of these types of policies with repeating stories. The agent or broker would claim that the policy would not only protect the client's family from a premature death but would also provide a lifetime tax-free income during their retirement years. It's quite common to see annual premiums of $75,000 to $100,000 go into these policies. Imagine the smile on these brokers' wallets when uninformed customers signed their documents.

There is much deception with these practices. Practices that have been prosecuted in the recent past. Some of the largest and most well-known insurance companies have had a history of deception dating back to the early 1980s, and in 1996 several were fined hundreds of millions of dollars for illegal practices with over one billion dollars in restitution payments, impacting tens of millions of policyholders in over 30 states. In 2016, both a major US bank and insurance company colluded to sell unwanted life insurance and annuities to their customers. They were drafting premiums from dormant bank accounts and forging signatures on insurance applications without the customers' knowledge! I would suggest that you never take the sales recommendation of an insurance agent or broker. I highly recommend always having an independent third-party advisor review all insurance-related recommendations to you.

All of these institutions, which most of us trust to help us protect our money and grow our savings, have a serious conflict of interest. Financial institutions shouldn't charge transaction fees when you purchase insurance or investments, change your investments, or move money from one account to another. They shouldn't be able to move clients into new accounts or products that generate higher fees for the firm than the existing account did. Earning transaction-based compensation on wealth advice is immoral—it reflects the fact that their real goal is not to help you achieve your dreams; it's to keep the transaction train in motion to pad their profits. Under this system, it doesn't matter whether your investments are rising or falling. The financial ruling class wins either way.

Here's an example: in early 2018, the US economy looked shaky. Global trade wars were heating up, the Fed was continuing to ratchet up interest rates, the tech industry was dealing with data privacy concerns, Great Britain was struggling with the implications of the Brexit vote, and North Korea was negotiating with the White House for a Presidential summit. The S&P 500 stock index recorded a decline for the first quarter of 2018, but one major investment firm (you'd recognize the name) couldn't have been happier. The firm declared that their year was off to a "good start" as the firm's first quarter net income jumped 35% to $8.7 billion. The biggest source of growth, unsurprisingly, came from equity sales and stock trading, which was 25% higher on the year. Fixed income, currency, and commodity trading increased by 7%.

That's the power of money in motion. Political and economic uncertainty was stimulating a lot of buying and selling. It didn't matter to the enormous investment firm and other big Financial Street institutions which products were being bought or sold, as long as the trades kept coming. That's why they rely on their army of salespeople to maximize transactions and new products.

I know what it's like to be a part of this army of salespeople. I was once on the frontlines, and I understand the pressures and the motivations. In 1989, with eight years in the financial services field already under my belt, I joined a major Wall Street investment management firm. I was young and full of optimism about my career. In my mind, I was in the business of helping people.

Even though I'd had my securities license for about five years, an insurance license for eight years, and had worked for a regional financial planning firm for six years, the firm asked me to sit through a training session—where I soon learned that this firm had other ideas about our role. During my orientation from the home office in Baltimore, a supervisor gave all the newly hired brokers a New York City phonebook and told us to start making calls. Obviously, we didn't know anything about these people or their needs and goals, so we were taught to kick off the conversation by asking, "Do you need income or growth?"

While this might seem like a legitimate question for an investment representative to ask, it's completely disingenuous in this situation. Most people don't know whether they need income or growth, and a good advisor can't answer that question until they understand their client's unique circumstances. Asking people cold whether they needed income or growth was a sales tactic designed to steer people into a conversation to get them to buy a particular product—for which we'd naturally receive a nice commission. We weren't being trained to effectively harness all of a client's valuable resources in the very best way in order to accomplish their most coveted aspirations—we were dialing for dollars.

The unveiling of this company's morals got worse with my tenure at the firm. Every week, the office manager would rank the brokers according to how much we'd earned in commissions, and he'd honor with a toast and a gift card to the broker with the highest total. Most weeks, the champion was the same guy. I'll call him Charlie. Charlie was a perfectly normal-looking guy in his fifties, but his work habits seemed like those of a mad scientist to us. He kept mostly to himself but clearly had a system that was working well for him—and that he certainly wasn't going to share with the rest of us.

One day, I walked by Charlie's office and got a hint about why he remained atop the sales figures week after week. I heard him promising a young couple that he could get them 20% returns on their portfolio. Talk about a sales pitch. Never mind that 20% is an unrealistic figure for long-term returns, it was the promise that really caught my attention. Advisors can't promise, in good faith, anything related to returns. We can't predict or control the future. What we can do is promise to always act in our clients' best interest. And we can look at historical returns, estimate the future performance of certain assets, and give our clients an idea of the range of outcomes they can expect through various timeframes. To go beyond this—to promise returns of a certain level—is to inspire false confidence in our clients. Charlie was taking advantage of this confidence to collect transaction fees. Yet here he was, receiving praise and awards from our sales manager week after week.

Then one Monday morning, our manager abruptly announced that Charlie was no longer with the firm. What happened? It soon came to light that Charlie had been fired and was facing a lawsuit from a client. He'd secretly been margin trading on all his client accounts—in other words, taking out loans inside those accounts without his clients' permission, but which allowed him to buy about twice as many shares as his clients could afford with their own money. Buying more shares earned him higher commissions, and clients didn't notice when stock prices were modestly rising. But when the 1990 to 1991 Gulf War recession hit and the value of those stocks fell big time, clients had to pay back those loans using the money in their brokerage accounts from the sale of stocks now at a depressed price. One of his victims was a 78-year-old widow who saw 80% of her savings evaporate in just months. Meanwhile, the manager who praised this scheme while it was happening kept his job and held on to the bonuses he earned from Charlie's criminal activity. Just where was the managerial oversight?

Charlie's methods were extreme, but they were a natural extension of the training he'd undergone and the environment in which he worked. Brokers get rewarded for bringing people and assets into the system and encouraging transactions of any kind. They're conditioned, even pressured, to produce revenues for the firm and themselves. They over-promote the attributes of the product they are pushing while minimizing or not even discussing the potential side effects or downside risks. And the sales recommendation is often in a silo, disregarding its overall fit within what should be a holistic wealth management plan.

An insurance or investment broker can be quite convincing during their sales pitch. You, the customer, fall prey to react in fear of missing out (FOMO) on possible profits or in fear of losing your money if the product isn't bought to protect it. Brokers' judgments and recommendations are blinded by their need to climb the ladder and please management along the way. They are fraught with conflicts of interest. The highest and best interest of the customer is left out of the equation when in fact it should be the whole equation.

The problem is made worse by the legacy model of "wealth management" that most people count on for support. As your life and finances become more complex, most people end up with a completely fragmented network of financial advice. It's not uncommon for a family to accumulate multiple investment brokers, insurance agents, accountants, lawyers, and financial planners who don't communicate with each other. Each one has their own limited picture of the family's needs and their own agendas and interests at stake. Even well-intentioned providers may be working at cross-purposes because they have no sense of your comprehensive financial picture. When your financial advisor and your accountant aren't working in collaboration, they might be missing out on a chance to optimize your tax situation. Charitable giving, Roth conversions, portfolio tax *loss* harvesting, and perhaps income management as it relates to Social Security taxation, Medicare premiums, or the Affordable Care Act premiums are just a couple of the potential benefits from year-end planning that require input from your entire team of professionals. When your lawyer isn't in communication with your wealth management team, which includes insurance coverage, your estate plan might suffer.

I've seen just how damaging it can be when you don't have an integrated team of advisors collaborating from a shared perspective of your needs. Several years ago, a longtime client I'll refer to as Dr. Henry called to let me know his father had passed away. Dr. Henry was one of five siblings, all of whom were cardiologists, like their father. He was the executor of his father's affairs, and he wanted to know what he could expect to face in the coming days and weeks ahead. He told me that his mother and father had accumulated more than $11 million in several investment accounts with two nationally prominent custodians and in addition had several large real estate holdings. Their asset values were segregated roughly equally in his mother's and father's holdings. Several years earlier, they had hired attorneys from a highly reputable firm to draft revocable trust documents with the intention of placing all their investment and real estate holdings into the trusts. With the revocable trusts, each parent would be able to control who the assets would transfer to and when they would transfer. The trusts would also allow the family to avoid the publicity, the hefty costs, and lengthy time delays associated with probate.

I told Dr. Henry that, based on what he was telling me, all seemed to be set up for a simple transfer of his father's holdings. As the executor, he should be able to settle his father's estate without much assistance or costs. If everything had been set up properly, all the assets would settle in the accounts of the benefactors in a matter of a few weeks.

There was just one glitch. It soon became known that the attorneys had failed to follow through to ensure that his parents' investment accounts and real estate holdings had been transferred to the revocable trusts. All of these assets were still titled in the name of the parents—not the trusts. Then the estate had to go through probate. And some very important transfer wishes went unfulfilled. There were substantial probate fees—and it took over 20 months and many long-distance trips for Dr. Henry to affect the transfer of all the assets into the interests of the beneficiaries. This was an unforced error, one that was easily controllable, that added to the stress and grieving of this beautiful family.

Stories like this are common because trying to coordinate your wealth affairs with unaffiliated advisors is almost always harmful to a family's financial net worth—and that's not to mention the undue stress and confusion it creates. With so much outside of your control, it's critical to control everything you can when it comes to wealth management—which is mostly your own behavior and the strategy you follow to pursue your lifetime intentional desires. One of the best ways to control those elements is to work with an advisory team who oversees all the financial details of your life with a deep understanding of the unique experiences, habits, and biases that have formed your relationship with money. I'll talk more about this approach in the second half of this book. For now, it's enough to understand that wealth management advice coming from multiple places at once almost certainly isn't going to align with your big-picture needs. In fact, as I said already, it's often the case that financial professionals don't care if their advice aligns with your needs. They're thinking about meeting firm quotas first, then providing for themselves, and then their customers.

By now you might be asking yourself where the regulators are in this picture. Unfortunately, a lot of the self-interested— sometimes illegal and oftentimes deceptive—behavior of financial professionals is sanctioned by the organizations you might think are protecting you. Take the Financial Industry Regulatory Authority, or FINRA. It's a government-authorized private corporation acting as a self-regulatory organization (SRO) charged with protecting investors by making sure the US securities industry and their brokers operate fairly and honestly. Disputes between consumers and brokers are typically handled through arbitration rather than litigation through the court system. This is because account opening agreements will almost always contain a provision binding the parties to arbitration in the event of a dispute. FINRA does provide some important services for investors, including background information for individuals in the financial services industry serving the public on BrokerCheck. finra.org. This online database offers a quick way to screen brokers and most recently investment advisors regulated by the Securities Exchange Commission, or SEC, before investing any money with them. This background check lists, among other items, any regulatory violations or filed customer complaints that might be on a broker's record.

FINRA's effectiveness is limited, however, because the organization works on behalf of the brokers it's supposed to regulate. It has a vested interest in keeping these brokers in business since its very existence depends on the success of those brokers as a collective body. Meanwhile, ordinary investors are left to fend for themselves in an environment designed to create chaos and sow confusion.

One of the driving factors behind this confusion is an ill-defined guideline known as the "suitability standard." The suitability standard, set by FINRA, requires only that brokers make recommendations that are "suitable" for customers. This is the standard that applies to brokers who work for big firms like Merrill, JP Morgan, Raymond James, Wells Fargo, Morgan Stanley, UBS, etc. What does "suitable" mean exactly? It's one of those words that's wide open to interpretation—and this is exactly why brokers love the suitability standard. Virtually any decision a broker makes on behalf of their client can be interpreted as "suitable," whether or not it's truly in the customer's best interest. Brokers are free to make very suboptimal recommendations for their clients' money, collect extravagant fees, and worse, as long as they can twist these sales recommendations to fall under the definition of "suitable." They are not required to present the full array of options that meet their customers' needs and situation. In fact, they're incentivized to sell their own products rather than competing products that might better suit their customers. From their perspective, the suitability standard boils down to this: "If my customer can absorb a potential financial loss from a recommendation I make on their behalf, that investment is suitable."

Fortunately, the prevailing Financial Street model isn't the only way to gain access to the financial markets and the power of innovation and creativity of Capitalism. Not all financial representatives are self-interested salespeople—some are actually paid to work for you rather than for their employers. Registered investment advisors (versus brokers) are not regulated by FINRA but by the Securities and Exchange Commission (SEC). They're also called "fiduciaries" because they are required to always place their clients' interests above their own. Instead of being governed by the suitability standard, they must follow the fiduciary standard, which is a specific set of guidelines laid out by the Investment Advisers Act of 1940. These guidelines forbid advisors from making trades that result in higher commissions for themselves, and they require advisors to give advice using the most accurate information and thorough analysis possible. Seek out a **FEE ONLY** financial advisory team. Their most common compensation method is to charge based on the assets under management, but they may charge based on a subscription fee schedule, an hourly rate, or an a la carte charge for specific services rendered. And their fees may cover services performed beyond the scope of just portfolio management.

A wealth advisory **TEAM** will also include and consist of a collaborative group of multi-disciplinary professionals providing formal financial planning, estate planning, insurance planning, accounting, which includes performing tax returns, and behavioral coaching under this one fee. There are no transaction-related or commission-related sales charges of any kind for the sales of products or the movement of monies and assets from any wealth recommendations. The client's interests are first in line.

I need to state a caveat here. I've discussed above how the majority of the financial representatives that you come into contact with for financial advice are really product salespeople earning commissions. This creates an inherent conflict of interest. I've also laid out a way to access wealth advice aligned with your interest, without these conflicts, through the relationship of a fee-only advisory team. As regulations stand today, financial representatives can hold licenses to be both brokers and fiduciaries. From an industry standpoint they are called "hybrid advisors" for this reason. But from a consumer standpoint, you would never know.

According to FINRA data, as of December 31, 2021, there are 304,867 individuals solely registered as an investment broker earning commissions only. THere are also 307,599 (hybrid) dually registered investment broker-investment advisors who earn commissions and fees. This compares to only 77,468 individuals solely registered as investment advisors that are compensated by fees only. The waters get murkier when you consider that according to the Insurance Information Institute (III), there were approximately 911,400 licensed life and health insurance brokers in the US at year end of 2021. You don't want to engage with parties that can be both an investment broker and a fiduciary. And you don't want to engage with parties that can be both an insurance broker and a fiduciary. These relationships are easy to sort out if you know how. Simply ask your advisory team candidate these questions: do you hold an insurance license? Do you hold FINRA licenses? If either answer is yes, keep looking. The only financial license your advisory team should have is issued by the SEC, and it is a Series 65 license.

Finding a fiduciary who will work for you rather than salespeople who work for their employers and themselves is a crucial step toward escaping Financial Street's predatory model. You'll have a trusted partner and ally as you work toward meeting your financial goals. The best fiduciaries, moreover, will take an active interest in your life as a whole. They'll try to understand the conscious and subconscious motives that underlie your financial goal setting and decision making.

To make the most of your partnership, you'll be an equally active participant in the process. You'll do the work of uncovering your authentic self and cultivating a more mindful presence. Remember how I described all the ways you've been hypnotized by your environment? Now it's time to learn how to start the process of de-hypnotization—of facing up to your deepest truths and rejecting the attitudes, beliefs, and outdated systems that don't serve you. Through this process, you can start to rewire your brain and develop habits that lead to a truly fulfilling and luminous life.

CHAPTER 4 LUMINOUS INSIGHTS

Through the centuries a financial industry of middlemen was created to assist consumers in gaining participation in owning securities of publicly traded companies with their surplus savings. As this industry of intermediaries evolved, it became expert at understanding its customers and their psyche. Like a puppeteer, they learned to manipulate the consumer to react to its elaborately constructed sales agenda. They mastered language and stories to sell their products and services. It is an industry that severely lacks integrity and a moral code, and is fraught with conflicts of interest.

Fortunately, there is an investing alternative that is aligned with your best interest and values. There is a growing legion of professionals called "registered investment advisors" that are regulated by the Securities and Exchange Commission who place your personal and financial interest ahead of theirs. They are not product salespeople, they are advisors. Seek out a FEE ONLY financial advisor for your wealth management relationship.

The ultimate way for any consumer to pave the way for a successful lifetime wealth journey is to hire a wealth advisory TEAM, which will consist of a diversified group of collaborating professionals with expertise in financial planning, insurance, investment, accounting, estate planning, and behavioral coaching, along with mind-body-spirit practices. The cocktail party question should be, "Who is your wealth advisory team?" instead of, "What's your investment broker's hot stock tip?"

CONTEMPLATIONS

- To what extent do you understand that there is a difference between Financial Street (the financial systems' middlemen) and Capitalism?
- To what extent do you know the difference between a financial broker and a fiduciary?
- Have you developed a master financial plan and visited it once a year with your team of advisors? If not, why not?
- How have you collected your needed providers of financial services over the years—randomly or intentionally? Did they seek you out or did you seek them out?

- Are they fee-only advisory professionals?
- Do any have licenses that could earn them a commission on investment or insurance product recommendations? If you don't know, ask them.
- To what extent do the providers of your financial services communicate with one another throughout the year? Do they even know who is on your team?
- Are they philosophically aligned? Do they all gather with you in the fall to maximize your year-end wealth strategies?
- Does the team you have assembled instill confidence in you achieving your non-financial and financial goals?
- If not, take some time to seek out a wealth advisory team. Interview two or three firms. Contact the firm I founded in Winston-Salem, North Carolina, Timonier, and use them as a benchmark for your search. You may also email me for any updates to available resources at Tim@LuminousWealth.com.

PART TWO

EMBRACING YOUR BEST SELF: HOW A DIFFERENT MODEL OF WEALTH MANAGEMENT CAN HELP YOU ACHIEVE YOUR GOALS WITH EASE AND GRACE

We need to develop and disseminate an entirely new paradigm and practice of collaboration that supersedes the traditional silos that have divided governments, philanthropies and private enterprises for decades and replace it with networks of partnerships working together to create a globally prosperous society.
—SIMON MAINWARING, AUTHOR

CHAPTER 5

TRANSCENDING THE OLD PARADIGM, STEP 1: CULTIVATING AWARENESS

If you want to judge your progress, ask yourself these questions: Am I more loving? Is my judgement sounder? Do I have more energy? Can my mind remain calm under provocation? Am I free from the conditioning of anger, fear, and greed? Spiritual awareness reveals itself as eloquently in character development and self-less action as in mystical states.

—EKNATH EASWARAN, SPIRITUAL TEACHER AND AUTHOR

I F YOU WANT TO KNOW how centered you really are, how anchored you are in your own mind and body, try driving for 10.5 hours and completing that drive on a lengthy, crowded six-lane highway. For a long time, I did that twice a week, shuttling back and forth between my homes in Winston-Salem, North Carolina, and West Palm Beach, Florida. It's a busy and chaotic stretch of road. Drivers down there range from the putzers in the far left-hand lane to adrenaline junkies going 110 miles per hour, swerving in and out of traffic without signaling. If you're not alert, you might get wiped out. On the other hand, if you don't stay calm, you're liable to take personally every reckless decision made by surrounding drivers.

I used these drives to test my inner state of being, to make sure I was in a place of positive energy and steady awareness. And I can honestly say that, more often than not, I was in that place.

I haven't always been, though. My spiritual journey has been a long one, and it hasn't moved in a straight line. It starts back when I was very young and continues to this day. Going down the spiritual path is a lifelong process for all. It's a moment-by-moment conscious awareness.

I grew up in Hampton, Virginia, and enjoyed a safe, comfortable upbringing that provided a model for the sanctuary I've sought to create for myself and others throughout my adult life. My parents were good, upstanding, middle-class Americans. They lived beneath their means and provided all the material, social, religious, athletic, and educational opportunities my two brothers and I needed for an enjoyable and balanced life. They gave back to their community with a lifetime of charity and volunteering. You could say it was a *Leave It to Beaver*-type family—with, not surprisingly, occasional disruptions introduced by the three boys.

We lived one house down from a Methodist church. My mother was a Sunday school teacher there and had perfect attendance for 21 years. For my mother, the church was her truth and a sanctuary. To me, though, it felt like a dungeon. The rituals, the lectures, and the heaven and hell story just didn't resonate with me. I felt fear and judgment. I know that's not how everyone experiences church—many find it a source of profound spiritual fulfillment, and I honor all paths that lead people to recognize themselves as part of something bigger and more connected than our mortal bodies. But that was not the experience I had in the church I grew up in, and this feeling colored my perspective toward spirituality during the early years of my life.

Then, in my early adulthood, after having three children of my own, my older brother committed suicide. I was devastated. It was the first tragic death in my immediate family, and it pushed me further away from my parents' church. At my brother's funeral, the preacher stood over his grave in sadness and indicated that due to the way my brother took his life, he would not be able to enter the Kingdom of Heaven. That hurt. I felt deep within myself that I couldn't participate in a way of thinking that condemned troubled souls to an eternity of torment.

That experience, combined with other experiences of disconnect with my religious upbringing, created a spiritual void in my life. For several years I focused on navigating the human condition of separateness and surviving the rat race most of us get caught up in when nurturing a growing family and building a career.

I didn't feel connected to the cosmos, nature, or humankind. I was an isolated being. From time to time, I did experience forces bigger than myself at work both within me and in the world at large. The summer when I felt with absolute certainty that I would win all of the major golf tournaments on the calendar is one example of that feeling. But it came and went, leaving me with a hunger for more. A deeper understanding. A more profound experience.

Then, when I was 38, I came across a book by Deepak Chopra called *Ageless Body, Timeless Mind.* Toward the end of the book, there was a single paragraph about meditation. Silence is the great teacher, Chopra explained, and to learn its lessons, you must pay attention to it. He quoted the great Sufi poet Rumi, who wrote, "Only let the moving waters calm down, and the sun and moon will be reflected on the surface of your Being." These words resonated with my soul. I was inspired by the idea of turning inward. I didn't have much to go on, so I devised my own meditation practice, sitting upright on the hearth of my fireplace for half an hour after work every day, eyes closed, staring at the back of my eyelids and repeating to myself, "Thy will be done."

I started reading more about meditation, and each insight I gained made me want to learn more. I found a teacher in Bedford, Virginia—a couple of hours away from Winston-Salem—and went there for three days to learn about something called "primordial sound meditation." This ancient technique, passed down from Indian rishis over thousands of years, involves repeating a three-word mantra as you meditate. The middle mantra is personalized according to your birthplace and time of birth. It's a sacred part of the practice, and sharing it with others is discouraged, but I will share with you the first and last words to my mantra: "Om … [sacred word] … Namaha." I still use this mantra today, repeating these words in the background of my mind while I sit comfortably in silence for an hour or so each day. In the early moments of a meditation, when my mind is often still swarming with thoughts, this mantra brings me back to center just as an automobile's GPS system will put you back on course to a far-off destination.

I've explored lots of different kinds of meditation over the years, and while they all provide different experiences, the benefits are largely the same. The word meditation means "becoming familiar with." Familiar with what? Familiar with the light that is incarnated into this physical body. Through mediation, you return to your original light and wholeness. All 60 trillion of the cells that make up your body return towards homeostasis, bringing your body and mind into balance. With meditation your mind quiets and allows you to become more settled in your body. It lowers your stress. It can allow you to be less judgmental. You become an observer of your own inner state, which helps you avoid getting caught up in emotional dramas. It puts you in touch with your eternal self, that part of you that transcends your day-to-day personality and is simply a form of energy, connected to all other beings and objects in the universe. After years of practice, I've noticed a host of concrete changes in myself: the cadence of my voice has changed, my body feels more centered, I've experienced physical healings, my thought process feels calmer, and I'm more aware and trustful of my intuition. My days are filled with synchronistic events and connections, and the desires that I have seem to manifest in an easier, accelerated timeline. I've experienced windows of time where I have reached a state of neutrality with my mind—completely calm and serene for a period of years. It felt as though I was simply an objective observer outside of my body, witnessing the actions and feelings of someone named Tim.

I can say that achieving this state of being is not a destination, but one of a journey. The weightiness of humanity and its dramas can pull you back into being a fully human participant. For all but a very few, one must carve out time in their day intentionally connecting with their higher self in order to master the mind and, thus, their life. And that's the challenge, isn't it? To find that daily time for devotion away from the busy-ness of family, friends, work, and life that is so needed in order to experience the best we can be. The nectar is worth it.

I talked earlier about how, for the first seven years of our life, our mind is like a sponge, soaking up everything around it without the filter we acquire as we grow older. Another way to think about this is in terms of brain waves. Neuroscientists have identified five types of brain waves—electrical impulses produced by the firing of our neurons. Throughout the day, our brains emit different kinds of waves, depending on what we're doing and how we're reacting to our environment. During most of our waking hours, we're sending off a lot of high-frequency beta waves, which help us form language, solve problems, and accomplish other high-level cognitive tasks. But beta waves are also associated with stress and anxiety. Meditation allows us to access lower-frequency alpha, theta, and even delta waves, which are associated with relaxed, open states, like those we enter into when we're daydreaming or about to fall asleep. When our brains are sending off more of these waves, we tend to be calmer, more content, and able to make more discerning choices.

I certainly experienced these feelings when I started meditating. I also experienced something even more dramatic. Nine months before I started meditating, I was playing golf at a country club with a few good friends. On the fourteenth hole I swung my driver and felt a pinch in my left shoulder. Actually, it was more like a knife stab. I had to walk off the course, and when I got back home, I couldn't even put on my suit coat, much less do more strenuous exercise like lifting weights. The pain didn't go away in the ensuing days and weeks.

I went to a physical therapist who beat and pulled on my shoulder, to no avail. I went to the personal trainer of the great tennis player Martina Navratilova, where I received electronic needle acupuncture. Those sessions felt good in the moment, but they didn't provide a permanent fix to my shoulder issue. Finally, I went to an orthopedic physician, who gave me a shot of cortisone with a needle several inches long. He told me to ice down my shoulder for two weeks, and if it didn't feel better, he would perform surgery, scraping out the underside of my shoulder socket to create space in the area of the initial impingement. I had no relief after my two-week protocol—but I was not about to go under the knife.

I continued to ice down my shoulder every night for the next nine months. I wasn't able to perform upper body weight training, I wasn't wearing business jackets, and there was a constant dull pain in my left shoulder at all times of the day.

When I made my journey to Bedford, Virginia, to learn about primordial sound meditation, I wasn't looking for any benefits to my shoulder. I simply wanted to know how to do it, to understand the technique and experience what it felt like. On the third day after returning to Winston-Salem, I was driving home from work after completing my afternoon hour-long meditation in my office chair. Suddenly, I realized that dull pain in my shoulder I'd grown so accustomed to was gone. It was one of the most intense feelings of relief I've ever had. I went back to my normal workouts, wearing suit coats, and playing golf on occasion. It's now been more than 26 years since my injury, and I have not had any issues since.

I can't promise that meditation will cure you of all your ailments, but I can say with confidence that those who practice it regularly become more conscious of their thoughts, their desires, their decisions, and the world around them. Even more transformational, it's a process that allows you to manifest your intentions for your highest good. It's like an incubator and processor to source energy.

In my case, a few months after I started meditating, I left my position as a financial advisor with a well-known national company and started my own wealth management firm, Baker Capital Advisors, Ltd. which years later was renamed to Timonier (pronounced *tee-mo-nyae*). I saw a need for a different wealth management model that took the whole person into account when making financial decisions, one that saw clients' financial success not as an achievement in itself but as a part of their overall happiness and well-being. And so, feeling newly centered and in control of my environment, I began to manifest my vision of providing a sanctuary for families, a safe haven where they could express their dreams and trust in a team of collaborative experts aligned to turn their aspirations into reality.

My spiritual foundation has sustained me during the past few decades, not only through times of happiness and smooth sailing but during moments of crisis. The deepest of these crises came in 2005, when my daughter, Constance, who was 21, lost her life in an auto accident while driving to see her college boyfriend. My world shattered. It was like looking into a clear nighttime sky and there were no reflections off the moon, no stars, no light. At the same time, I felt that the universe was trying to say something to me. The day before her accident, we had spent the entire day together in Columbia, South Carolina, where she was attending college. It was an extraordinary day of togetherness and conversation, and we connected as deeply as we ever had during her short life.

After her passing, I decided to put back on my calendar an event that I'd canceled earlier in the year: a tour of Indian temples led by a partner of Deepak Chopra's, Roger Gabriel. The tour came on the heels of a meditation course taught by Chopra, and that trip, which I took at the beginning of 2006, allowed me to begin to process not only my daughter's passing, but everything that was going on in my work and life.

Still, I felt all the pain and anguish that any parent would feel upon the death of a beloved child. Everyone has their own way of processing tragedy. Without counseling or leaning on family or friends, I simply cried until I couldn't cry anymore. One day as I walked past my daughter's photo on the way to breakfast, I noticed that instead of feeling a tear run down the side of my face, I smiled. That was three years after her death. Throughout this period of grieving, though, I kept up my daily meditation practice, and it kept me centered and grateful for what I had—which was still a lot. I had been gifted 21 years to witness the amazing life and light of a beautiful daughter. Her passing positively transformed many lives who awoke inspired by the touch she had on their hearts. Her light continues to support North Carolina families with scholarships to her alma mater in her memory.

Whether you are 21 or 121, when you leave this body, the passage of time is that of a blink of an eye. The length of your life doesn't define its wealth of living. Constance Arielle Baker's was rich and left an impactful legacy. To have my child leave this earth before me wasn't in accordance with the way I was told the world would work. But ever so slowly and consistently, bits of new light came into my vision, until at some point I discovered I had formed a new worldview. It was as if I were reborn. I had gone through the portal of transcendence and returned. It happened not in the conventional way, by walking down a church aisle asking forgiveness and declaring my faith, but through undergoing my own experience of light dawning from the shadows of darkness. After that, I lived my life from a wide middle path, never succumbing to emotional highs or lows. It was a very serene and peaceful place. A place where I felt I was an objective observer of my own life. I'm not saying I don't encounter emotional disturbances from time to time, but I'm always able to return to this central state of tranquility, ease, and grace.

It's from this place that I provide clients an outer experience of calm and confidence. But it's up to you to develop an inner experience that keeps you centered throughout the inevitable turbulence of life. I encourage anyone who's moved to do so to explore meditation as a way to cultivate awareness of yourself and your environment. Meditation isn't a religion. In fact, you can incorporate meditation into your own spiritual and religious beliefs. It can be the vibrational caretaker for your mind and body temple. I know not everyone will take the same path I did, nor should they. I offer my story not as a prescription, but as a demonstration of how personal every spiritual journey is.

There are countless paths to cultivating awareness, and different people will respond to different practices. The only requirement is that you make a commitment to your practice and allow its effects to unfold over time. I've seen folks have great success with prayer, de-hypnotization (getting rid of the programs you've unconsciously downloaded from your environment), breathwork practices, neuro-linguistic programming (a set of language-based interventions in your behavioral patterns), mindful affirmations, and a number of other activities that pull us out of our habitual ways of being and allow us to see the world more objectively.

I encourage you to experiment with different approaches and see what resonates with you. Keep in mind, though: while some effects of practices like meditation can be immediate and powerful, in the vast majority of cases, your life won't change all at once. A spiritual journey, like a financial journey, is a lifetime commitment, and it takes time and discipline to achieve the deepest benefits. Moreover, once you start feeling those benefits, you can't just stop—it's a continuous, never-ending process, with inevitable frustrations and hiccups along the way. I understand that not everyone will want to pursue such a path. You can't force it. And even if you do feel called toward a spiritual practice, you may feel emotionally challenged to spend years working on yourself before the benefits of greater awareness begin to pay off.

Fortunately, there are two actions you can take right now to set yourself on a more personally fulfilling track in life—and improving your relationship with money, investing, and habits of well-being can be a big part of that change.

ACTION #1. DISCOVER YOUR BIASES AND PATTERNS.

As in all realms of life, your beliefs about money shape your experience with it. Change your beliefs and perceptions, and you can change your behavior—and achieve more satisfactory outcomes. The problem is, many of our beliefs are buried deep in our subconscious minds, so deeply ingrained that we don't even realize they're there. That's exactly what a bias is: a hidden belief. Fire doesn't know itself to be hot, a knife doesn't know itself to be sharp, and water doesn't know itself to be wet. Likewise, while we see the effects of our biases all the time in our actions and emotional responses, many of us never take the time to identify the biases themselves, much less take the necessary next step of uncovering their root causes.

Here's an example of how a bias can have a huge effect on your financial life—and, by extension, your life in general. A few years ago, a client came into my office and announced that she wanted to make an offer on a beach property. She was in her early fifties, and she was doing fine financially but wasn't well-off enough to put in an offer on a second home. I thought she knew this too because she and I had discussed a beach house as a long-term goal, something she could aim for close to or in retirement. But retirement was still a long way off for her. What changed?

It turned out that she'd come into some money earlier than expected. Her mother had passed away due to an unexpected illness, and my client had inherited a few hundred thousand dollars. That sounds like a lot, but if you want to live on a financial drawdown from your one-million-dollar globally diversified portfolio that is not only sustainable but able to keep pace with inflation, you should expect to receive about $3,750 in monthly gross income. It takes a lot of assets to comfortably provide the lifestyles we are seeking. I doubted whether the new influx of money at this time could justify the purchase of an expensive second home, one that would add additional monthly expenses to the budget. Soon enough, my team's research bore this out. But my client was afflicted with a bias I like to call "sudden money syndrome." She'd come across a chunk of money and couldn't wait to spend it, whether or not it made sense in the grand scheme of

65

her master financial plan. She'd gotten caught up in the emotions of the moment and allowed them to determine her actions.

I sensed a deeper force at work as well. For this client, as with most people who suffer from sudden money syndrome, it wasn't in her subconscious conditioning to have the level of wealth that she'd come into. She didn't grow up in an environment of financial abundance. It didn't line up with her sense of herself. She was feeling stressed and anxious. And so, her impulse was to match her outer circumstances with her inner being—to unload the money as quickly as possible so that she could go back to the financial state she'd been in before she received her inheritance. She enjoyed the new wealth, she "wanted" the wealth. But it wasn't who she was. She had not been given the tools to respect it in her life, and she had not trained herself to use it wisely. Remember—we don't get the outcome of what we want; we get the outcome of who we are.

Fortunately, over the course of the next few weeks, I was able to demonstrate to my client that it wouldn't be wise to make a hasty decision. The inheritance could accelerate her beach house purchase compared to our previous projections, and that was great news, but an immediate purchase risked endangering her long-term financial safety. More of life needed to unfold before big financial expenditures could be made.

In this case, I was able to identify my client's bias and take action against potential negative effects, but you can't make a long-term change unless you dig deeper and reveal what caused the bias to take root in the first place. I mentioned in Chapter 2, there's an entire field of economics, called "behavioral economics," that's largely concerned with labeling people's common biases related to money. Here are a few more examples: "loss aversion" (a preference for avoiding losses over acquiring gains), "recency bias" (believing that what's happened recently will continue to happen), and "illusion of control" (the tendency to overestimate the ability to control events). The value of behavioral economics is limited, though, because it only names the problems—it doesn't solve them. Telling someone that loss aversion is the reason they want to sell stocks and put their money into bonds (even though those bonds won't help them meet their long-term financial goals) doesn't affect their desire to go ahead and sell—just as showing someone where the gym is located doesn't help them lose weight.

For me, behavioral economics is analogous to Western medicine's focus on curing chronic diseases with pharmaceuticals. Typically, pharmaceuticals help alleviate symptoms, but they don't get to the root cause. In order to permanently eliminate the disease (the dis-ease), you must understand and heal its cause. Most often, that cause can be found in poor habits of nutrition and endlessly repeating negative and fearful mantras of the mind. Our biography becomes our biology. Combatting these ingrained habits requires a change of behavior, not surgery or a pill. Even prominent behavioral economists are coming around to this truth. Recent Nobel Prize winner Richard Thaler, who's best known for his work in behavioral economics, recently admitted, "I don't think I've changed anyone's mind in 40 years [by labeling their behavior]. You basically don't change minds."

What I'm inviting you to do is begin the process of becoming aware of the cause of your automatic responses. I talked a couple of chapters ago about the importance of your early childhood environment in the formation of beliefs and attitudes toward money, and this is usually a good place to look. Our ancestors' genes, our mother's emotional and physical state during the nine months we spent in her womb, the way we see our parents and other close family members react to life's challenges—all these play critical roles in the formation of our biases.

Traumatic events too can have a huge impact. I once had a client come to me whose big goal was to provide $10 million for each of his two daughters. He was already well-off—he had $4 million in investment portfolios—but that was a lot less than he needed. As it turned out, it was a lot less than he could have had too if he had invested from a place of clear intention rather than fear. What was up?

In an early conversation with him I found out that he had been kicked out of his house when he was 12 years old and had lived on the street for two years. The traumatic experience etched a groove deep into his subconscious, which expressed itself in two competing impulses: first, he wanted to make sure his daughters never felt emotionally or financially insecure; second, he'd dumped way more money than he should have into life insurance, rather than investing in growth assets that would have set him on a path toward his $20-million goal. His financial decisions were being ruled by an unconscious bias, and that bias had led him to sabotage his own best intentions.

Uncovering these biases on your own can be hard, which is why working with an objective partner can help. As a wealth manager, one of the first steps I take with a new client is to develop a personal genogram. A genogram is a representation of family relationships that allows clients to observe hereditary patterns and multi-generational influences in their own lives. I'll talk more about this work in the next chapter and how valuable it can be to explore the environmental factors that formed your worldview when you were young. Such an exploration does have its limits: much of your past may be lost to memory, and there may be no way of knowing for certain what our environment was teaching us while we were in the womb. For now, though, just keep in mind that as you explore the origins of your biases, your family and early childhood will likely prove to be a fertile starting point.

ACTION #2. DEVELOP PASSIONATE AND INSPIRING IDEAS.

Even if you can't identify all of the forces that shaped you, you can still take what you've learned about yourself and your biases and apply that knowledge to the creation of the life you want now—and that transcends into the future. It involves passionately dwelling on your desired outcomes and reshaping your belief system to align with those outcomes. You shape yourself from the inside out. If you want to create a new personal reality, you have to become a new personality. Repeating the same habits and patterns of thought of yesterday will keep you stuck in the past. Strive to awake each day focused on what you desire your life to be, then take new actions and hold new thoughts to manifest your outcome. You have to literally become someone else.

It's worth reiterating: beliefs shape experiences. This isn't some magical process. In fact, we see it happen all the time. If you see yourself as someone who's capable of rising to big challenges, you're more likely to project confidence in a job interview and get the job you want. If you believe you have a chance with that person you see across the room at a party, you're more likely to go over and talk to them—and ultimately end up with them. There's even evidence showing that middle-aged adults who have more positive beliefs about aging live an average of 7.5 years longer than those who hold more negative beliefs—and that includes controlling for risk factors and current health.

Outcomes are tied to beliefs. The two work together, helping to forge the reality that is your unique experience. It makes sense that identifying the outcomes you most deeply desire is a crucial part of stepping into the best version of yourself—and creating a master financial plan will help you get there. A couple of chapters ago, I demonstrated how asking the simple question, "What brings you joy?" had a transformational effect on the lives of a couple I was working with. That question is a wonderful starting point for developing passionate ideas. It can help you separate what is truly meaningful in your life from what you only think you want, the desires that are born from your environmental conditions.

This is the difference between conventional goal setting and authentic goal setting. It's so important not to base your decisions on other people's way of doing things. For example, I've worked with many clients who assume that it's automatically better to put their children in private school starting from kindergarten. They maintain this method of education through high school. While it's critical for our kids to experience the most constructive and loving environment through age seven, private school after that age isn't necessarily the best path for all. And, if you have more than one child, the bills become quite substantial. The result of that decision might not lead their kids to a more meaningful experience or getting into a better college, but it often leads to financial insufficiencies in areas of their lives that are closer to their hearts. In other words, by setting goals thoughtlessly, they're blocking the manifestation of their most passionate ideas. They're not allowing themselves to experience whatever it is that is more deeply and personally aligned with their truest selves.

The actions I've covered in this chapter are just the starting point for cultivating greater awareness and re-aligning your life. But the key word here is journey. The self-work I've been talking about is a lifetime process. Everyone must go at their own pace and follow their own path. I know from personal experience and working with thousands of individuals and families that some or even many of you may not be ready to embark on this journey. For those who are ready to take the first steps, understand that it will likely be quite some time before you feel fully aware of the subconscious forces driving your decisions. That's to be expected. When the student is ready, the teacher will be there. You will not miss out.

Wherever you are in your personal journey, you don't have to continue suffering from the effects of your biological and cultural inheritance. You can find a trustworthy partner who can help you feel immediate relief while also guiding you down the path toward a more authentic life. Let me tell you what this kind of partner looks like and the specific ways they can help you experience your aspirational dreams.

CHAPTER 5 LUMINOUS INSIGHTS

Through meditation, you return to your original light and wholeness. All 60 trillion of your body's cells return towards homeostasis, bringing your body and mind into balance. Harmony. A noble life is one with inner peace and outer fulfillment. There are two actions you can take to embark on aligning your inner world with your outer world. You can begin to recognize your biases and patterns that are not serving your highest good. These blind spots and repeating behaviors can sabotage your most passionate desires, especially in the area of money and investing. Embrace, but recognize when these entrenched friends arise; then pause and make a new choice. The second action is to develop worldly goals to match that of what you hold sacred. Contemplate how you want to "be" in the world. Align your sacred values with your passions and authentic desires. Then express your uniqueness and take actions, including in the area of investing, that match your value system. When you work with a financial planning team that takes your whole person into account, your financial success is not just an achievement in itself, but it becomes part of your overall happiness and well-being.

CONTEMPLATIONS

- Spend time contemplating the main aspects of your life that are serving you in the very best way and, more importantly, those parts of your life that you are not happy with. The ones that seem to be stuck in a repeating pattern or circumstance.

- See if you can identify the causal behavior or belief that enables these patterns to occur. This may be difficult. So, if you feel safe to do so, solicit a conversation for thought and feedback with a trusted companion who knows you quite well.

- Write down your sacred values. Then list those aspects of your life you have a passion for. They may even be aspects you have not been expressing. Begin to take new actions with your daily habits that will put into practice this new alignment of inner values and outer passions. It may be hard and uncomfortable in the beginning, but like anything in life, practice makes perfect.

CHAPTER 6

TRANSCENDING THE OLD PARADIGM, STEP 2: WORKING WITH A TRUSTED PARTNER

Trust is built when someone is vulnerable and not taken advantage of.
—BOB VANOUREK, AUTHOR OF *TRIPLE CROWN LEADERSHIP*

A FEW YEARS BACK, A PHYSICIAN scheduled a meeting at my office to discuss her new employer's 401(k), which I was managing. Her name was Kaitlin, and she was highly intelligent, emotionally mature, and organized. Among my many inquiries, I asked if she had any other retirement accounts that we should consider as we began formulating a base financial plan, our foundational platform for providing advice. She informed me she had eight separate IRAs, holding a total of about $1 million altogether.

That immediately set off an alarm bell: there's no reason for anyone to have eight retirement accounts. For one thing, with her level of earned income, it meant that she was prevented from implementing an annual IRA Roth conversion strategy, which could have allowed her to collect tax-free withdrawals in retirement. When she added that her advisor was planning to roll over another $350,000 from a prior employer's 403(b) plan and open three more IRAs, the alarm bell started blaring.

I asked for some time to review her account statements and to research the firm that had been providing the advice. What I found on the firm's website was appalling if not completely deceptive. Her advisor seemed legitimate at first glance. His homepage prominently advertised his many industry awards and accolades— one of this magazine's "Top 1,200 Advisors," one of that magazine's "Top 4,000 Advisors," etc.—and he was a registered fiduciary. But he failed to disclose that he also ran a commission-based securities firm. He was effectively a double agent, a broker posing as a fiduciary. After some deeper digging, I realized that he'd also failed to disclose several industry infractions and customer complaints. I found this information by going to BrokerCheck.finra.org, mentioned earlier, and filling in his name, so it wasn't a complete surprise when I soon discovered that he was collecting a much higher-than-usual fee for each of Kaitlin's IRAs.

This guy wasn't looking out for her best interests, to say the least. He didn't do any true financial planning with all the accountability, risk management, tax analysis, and estate planning that phrase entails. He'd even failed to notice—or didn't care— that three of Kaitlin's IRAs still named her ex-husband as the beneficiary. He talked a good game, and he had a slick website, but his actions and advice were not in alignment with fiduciary responsibilities and his website's presentation. He made things complicated and called them sophisticated. He'd been corrupted by greed, which is the flipside of fear. Likely he was afraid of not having enough money, of not having enough security, so he'd created money management systems to maximize his revenues at the expense of his trusting clients.

My recommendation for Kaitlin was to roll over all eight of her IRAs, as well as the 403(b) account from a previous employer, not to my firm's private wealth management services, but into her current employer's 401(k) plan. This move would give her global diversification within a set of low-cost asset class mutual funds, and it would reduce her fees to a quarter of what she was previously paying. Additionally, she then could begin funding a non-deductible traditional IRA, which she could in turn convert each year to a Roth IRA. She listened calmly as we laid out the discrepancy between her current plan and a potential path she could walk. She admitted that she was surprised. She said she had never had a problem with the advisory firm she was working with. They were friendly, attentive, and always treated her respectfully, or so it seemed. But now that she was being exposed to a new landscape of strategies, she could see how they'd taken advantage of her. She was ready to move forward with advisement that was in her interest. She was confident, clear, and took decisive steps in implementing her new plan.

Stories like this one illustrate why handing over the reins of your financial life to a financial advisor is such a serious matter. You're trusting a big part of yourself and your future to other people, so it's crucial to choose the right partners from the hundreds, if not thousands, available to you.

A couple of chapters ago, I explained the difference between brokers and fiduciaries: brokers, like the guy taking advantage of Kaitlin, tend to be self-interested salespeople, incentivized to provide recommendations that maximize their and their company's earnings—not yours. They follow guidelines designed to protect the industry—not you. Eventually, this practice will be eliminated. I just don't want you to get blindsided with it while it still exists. It can be very costly, not just in terms of your results, but in terms of what you'll bring forth to the next generation by virtue of your experience.

Fiduciaries, on the other hand, are required to place their clients' interests above their own. They must give advice based on the most accurate information and thorough analysis possible and are forbidden from making trades and recommendations that result in higher compensation for themselves. Their calling is to be of service. Their reward is their clients' happiness and success.

One of the best illustrations of differentiating the role of a broker versus a fiduciary was shared years ago by Elliott Weissbluth, former CEO of HighTower Advisors, using a storyboard video. His parable is priceless. He begins: when you walk into a butcher shop and ask the person behind the counter what to have for dinner this week, he might recommend burgers, a rib eye, a skirt steak, maybe pork chops. In other words, he's going to recommend meat. He's a butcher, and he wants to sell you something from his case. Ask a dietician, on the other hand, and you'll have a totally different experience. Before answering, the dietician will probably start by asking questions about you—your age, weight, health status, exercise habits, your health goals, etc. They'll carefully consider all that information and develop recommendations based on your specific dietary needs. They might suggest salads, whole grains, fish, nuts—whatever they understand will be best for your long-term health.

Brokers are butchers; fiduciaries are dieticians. Brokers want to sell you a particular product while fiduciaries make recommendations based on a more holistic and objective view of what's truly best for you. Fiduciaries aren't trying to sell you anything. Instead, they're partnering with you to help you live your one best life.

That said, not all fiduciary advisors are the same. The best advisors step into their clients' shoes with the knowledge, experience, professional skills, and training to help them meet their deepest desires. In order to do this, advisors must know themselves as well—they must remain calm and anchored in even the most turbulent circumstances to act as a pause button for your life.

Let me go even further: the best fiduciaries "become" their clients. They harness all available intellectual resources to help their clients live with ease and grace as expressions of their singular selves. To do this, they must gain a deep and wide knowledge of their clients. They may even help the client discover who they really are.

What I'm really talking about here is the difference between portfolio management and wealth management. Most people, when they hear the phrase "financial advisor," think of someone concerned exclusively with shifting around investments to maximize marginal returns. In other words, they think of a portfolio manager. Portfolio management is important, but it's only one part of a more holistic practice of wealth management. Wealth management entails looking at all aspects of each client's financial picture—and expands beyond that to consider each client's overall well-being.

What does this kind of relationship look like at a personal level when you're pursuing your most important life goals? How does it translate into practical services and advice you should expect to receive? The best way I can answer that question is to share some of the most effective tools and methods I've used in my many years as a wealth advisor—and especially the model I developed when I founded my own firm. That's because I built my firm according to my idea of what an exemplary practice should look like.

All of life is a fractal—an infinite repeating pattern of information. You see it in the cosmos, you see it in nature, and you see it in the repeating patterns of behavior in human beings. That's why, several years ago, I began using assessment tools to reveal the personalities of our clients, the repeating patterns of qualities and attributes that serve them in a positive way as well as those characteristics, those biases, that are detrimental to their pursuit of fulfillment and joy. These assessment tools allow you to honor and embrace all of who you are. They provide insight into your true passions and the path that you are here to experience. Only through self-inquiry and an authentic discussion of your life's passions and goals can you forge a real relationship with an advisor.

Of course, wealth managers need to look deeply at all of your investments, bank accounts, retirement plans, insurance coverage, and spending habits—but the numbers aren't what's most important to you as you set a course to your harbor of destiny. You want a partner who takes the time to learn about you as a whole person: your family history, dreams, passions, fears, and all the deepest, most authentic aspects of your living self. Your financial life can't be separated from the other parts of your life. It's all interconnected. Making the best investment decisions requires a deep understanding of your current circumstances, the people surrounding you, and how you think and feel about who you are, your past as well as your future.

One tool that has proven especially useful to me over the years is called a Communication DNA Consumer Report. This assessment, developed by Hugh Massie, the founder of DNA Behavior in 2001, provides insights into how you like to be communicated with and your preferred learning style. For example, you might be an empathetic and open communicator who prefers to be spoken to in a relaxed and warm manner, as much in tune with the moods and emotions in a conversation or email exchange as you are in its informational content. Or you might prefer a more to-the-point communication style, interested mainly in facts, data, bottom-line resolutions, and ideas. Whatever your communication style, it's incumbent on the advisor to be able to relate to it in order to conduct meetings in harmony. The advisor has their own unique style and must adapt to conduct an effective meeting.

The communication tool has proven especially useful in revealing important, previously obscured differences in the communication styles within couples. For example, a few years ago I met with two partners who had very different communication preferences. The wife, Karen, was inherently very trusting. She was eager for our recommendations and didn't need to hear the logic behind them. Her husband, Terry, on the other hand, was more information-oriented and had a strong desire to absorb all the details of our planning process. I knew from the first time I met with this couple that I'd have to communicate with each partner very differently to reach them effectively. Here, more or less, is how I addressed them:

"I'd like for you to know that through our assessments, you both want to review our shared information today in different ways. Karen, I know you want to get to the bottom line of our recommendations and discover how they will impact your plans. And, Terry, I know you are going to need to hear the options considered, the pros and cons of those options, and the evidence behind our recommendations. So, Karen, please bear with me if it seems I'm getting a bit technical—and I will be equally mindful to your needs as well."

It's important to keep everyone engaged, but it's not always a perfect world. Recognizing different communication styles up front helps though. When you and your partner know your own preferences, you can better understand your conversations with each other and with your advisor. A Communication DNA Report helps short-circuit a lot of potential misunderstandings. It can even turn communication irritations into moments of levity.

Before I move on, I want to pause here and bring a special light to a systemic issue of the financial industry. Women have not been given the proper respect or attention that their spouses and male counterparts have been afforded. The male-dominated financial industry has been guilty of providing unequal attention and placation to their male constituents in an advisory relationship. Women are an equal, if not greater, value in the dynamic aspects of managing a family's household resources. A woman being ignored and left uneducated about the economics of life's possibilities is detrimental to the family's success and disrespectful to our valued partners. It makes no conscious sense. I would say to both men and women, if either of you sense a disparity of attention by your advisory relationship, make it known to that party. And if things don't change, leave.

The communication tool I just mentioned encourages even unconscious advisors to give equal importance and attention to each member of the couple in front of them. More women are entering lead roles in the wealth advisory space, but the industry is changing far too slowly. Look for advisory teams that are integrated with and strike a balance of feminine and masculine energy for a holistic experience. You have choices.

Another tool I strongly advocate is the Human Archetype Assessment. This questionnaire asks a series of questions designed to reveal your natural financial DNA—the key characteristics and tendencies that are hardwired in the way you think about and interact with your financial resources. Hugh Massie is also the mastermind behind this technology that is used in over 123 countries and utilized in many of the top universities in America as well as many well-known financial institutions and corporate HR departments.

This tool recognizes that some people are results-oriented, meaning they're laser-focused on outcomes while paying less attention to the process of getting there. Others are relationship-oriented, meaning the connections they form with people on the way toward meeting their goals is as important as particular outcomes. Some make decisions quickly while others move carefully, needing time to reflect on information. The assessment pinpoints which of the ten main behavior styles (called personas) you embody, from strategist to facilitator to reflective thinker and more. And taking this deep dive into a region of your subconscious makeup helps reveal both the supportive programming of your unique identity and the potential challenges and biases you may face while also helping your financial partners work with you more effectively.

Take my archetype: I'm an initiator. That means I like to take bold, aggressive actions. I prefer to create rules and set the agenda for others to follow. I'm goal-driven and tend to move quickly if possible. I'm not afraid to take on challenging tasks. As with all of the behavior styles, the characteristics of initiator are neither inherently positive nor inherently negative. I can harness my predilections to get things done quickly and effectively, making strong moves and thinking creatively to benefit myself and others. I'm open to new ideas and curious about the world around me. But I'm also prone to certain biases—for example, the "newness bias," which means I'm likely to give more weight to recent information and ideas—and I may find it difficult to follow set procedures or translate ideas to the concrete world.

The key is that I know all this about myself, and this knowledge allows me to recognize when my biases are arising and take a pause on my actions. It allows me to support the traits and response systems that serve me in a positive way while avoiding the unconscious reactions that might negatively impact me. Likewise, when I know my clients' inclinations, I can better help harness those traits that serve them well and protect them from blind spots and repeating patterns that don't.

These assessment tools are invaluable methods that have helped me get a basic understanding of my clients' personalities and the many aspects of behavioral tendencies. But that's just the beginning. To act as a true guide on your financial journey, advisors must explore the circumstances that made you into the person you are. I made sure to begin this process with clients at our very first meetings, which I call "discovery meetings." A good advisor will want to dig deep into your relationship with money. This means looking at much more than what's in your 401(k) plan. It's an investigation of all the current and future details of your financial life. What are your sources of income, and what are your expenditures? Do you have a desire for a second career? Do you have any possessions that you haven't even been thinking of as assets, like family heirlooms or art? Do you have a potential inheritance in your future, or, instead, are you expecting to provide assistance to parents or other family members?

Beyond these financial considerations, you want an advisor who's interested in your personal history, attitudes, and beliefs. One powerful tool in this effort is the development of the genogram that I mentioned in the last chapter. A genogram is a representation of family relationships that allows clients to observe hereditary patterns of thought and behavior and multi-generational influences in their own lives. To create a genogram for my clients, I ask detailed questions to learn what their parents and sometimes grandparents did for a living, what kind of health they were in, what kind of partnering patterns they had, their financial situation throughout their lives, and what messages they communicated to the client about money, both verbally and by example.

Every situation is different, and every person responds differently to the forces they encounter in their upbringing. People who came from poor homes can feel rich, and people who came from wealthy atmospheres can feel poor, neglected, or uninspired. The key is to understand each person's unique attitudes about the world they live in and their relationship with money. It's a bonus if the discussion identifies the root causes behind these attitudes, which were more than likely ingrained from their environment in the early years of development.

These conversations can become unexpectedly emotional for clients. About five years ago, I had a discovery meeting with a husband and wife who worked in the medical field—he was a radiologist, and she was a nurse anesthetist. After listening to her husband share his family's story, it was the wife's turn. Immediately I could tell that she was upset. She began by saying that her family enjoyed a lavish lifestyle in her early childhood years. They lived in the best neighborhood in town, employed staff to take care of the family and property, sent the kids to private school, and had all the luxuries you could imagine. Then the family fell on the hardest of times. Remembering this dramatic change in her circumstances brought tears and more tears. She was reliving the pain of having to move to an apartment, of leaving private school, of losing friends and self-esteem, as if it were happening again.

We gave her some time to recover and continued on with our conversation at her request. She had been living her whole life in shame and guilt, which she had hidden even from her husband. As we got into the family's finances, she revealed that her occupational income was twice what her husband had thought it was. Her retirement savings also were substantially more than what her husband had thought them to be. Her relationship with money was so painful that for years she had avoided discussing it with anyone, even her husband. She had completely swept all money matters under the rug.

After the meeting, her husband emailed me to thank me and say how valuable the conversation had been. He'd learned things about his wife's past, and her emotional life, that he wished he'd known before. Bringing to light that which had been covered up for years began the healing process. I'm happy to say that this uncovering has brought her a tremendous amount of relief, as expressed in the many encounters I've had with her and her family since then. She proceeded to carry a new sense of heightened levity each time she entered our offices.

That's just one example of how profound these conversations can get. They have allowed me to connect with clients on a human level, one that goes deeper than a typical professional relationship. In an ideal world, everyone would devote the time necessary to becoming more in tune with their minds and bodies and leading more intentional lives—all the difficult but rewarding self-work I talked about in the last chapter. For those who haven't taken those steps or who are in the process of taking them, a trusted financial partner can become your bridge to peace, centeredness, expanded awareness, and unexplored possibilities.

In this chapter I've focused on how important it is that your advisors know where you're coming from, but it's equally important for your advisor to know where you're going. Up next, let's explore how the entire arc of your life can play out in your advisor's office, from your earliest childhood to your visions of future fulfillment, and even extending to future generations.

CHAPTER 6 LUMINOUS INSIGHTS

For the consumer, the landscape for harnessing all of the needed wealth management services to run their life smoothly is fragmented and confusing. Financial Street is tainted with conflicts of interest, misaligned compensation arrangements, and personnel that lack integrity. However, the industry is beginning to mature. It may take some time to find, but there are a growing number of fee-only multi-family offices that are culturally aligned with your interest and values and, in fact, place your interest ahead of theirs.

Beyond making sure you are working with a fee-only advisory firm, make sure you are working with a fiduciary team that approaches their work from a holistic perspective. An exemplary firm will have human archetype assessment tools that will assist you in "knowing thyself." They will also be transparent in disclosing their own personas. This holistic approach frees you from your unconscious past, uncovers the authentic unique you, and aligns your resources to fulfill your heartfelt destiny.

CONTEMPLATIONS

- Do your wealth advisory relationships take the time to understand you and your family lineage in a holistic way? A way that understands that the non-financial aspects of you fully impact your wealth being?
- What was the direction of conversation when you were interviewing the critical caretakers of your wealth affairs?
- After initial greetings, was the focus of the meeting on your assets or on you? What about you were they interested in?
- What type of assessments were used to help your advisors understand your communication preference?
- Financial advisors are asked to "know their clients," but rarely do clients know themselves. What discovery process did your advisors use to reveal the real you?
- Do your advisors know how you feel about money and what your money scripts (your money beliefs) are? Do you? Perhaps you may write them down.
- Do you know those qualities and attributes that have long served to support your best life? Make a list of them.
- Do you know what biases and blind spots you have that don't serve you in the very best way? This answer most often is no. You will need an archetypal assessment or a gifted loved one to reveal the answer to this question.
- Do you recognize any debilitating patterns from your family lineage that affect your life? What are they?
- If you are a couple working with advisors, do they treat each of you with equal attention and respect?

If you haven't done so already, be sure to take advantage of the offer provided at the beginning of this book:

The Awakened Investor Assessment
For your convenience, below is the website link to take your
DNA Behavioral Identity Assessment
https://discovery.dnabehavior.com/investor/Luminous Wealth/1581/704

CHAPTER 7

THE HALLMARKS OF HOLISTIC WEALTH ADVISEMENT AND GUIDANCE

You never change things by fighting the existing reality. To change something, build a new model that makes the existing model obsolete.

—BUCKMINSTER FULLER

YOU'RE NOT IN CONTROL OF every aspect of your life. The circumstances you're born into, the actions of people around you, the decisions of political leaders, the weather—so much of your day-to-day experience is determined by forces outside of your personal volition, yet you still have so much power.

We all have power over the way we respond to both negative and positive events, and over the qualities in ourselves we express through our actions. By setting inspired intentions and pursuing them through conscious decisions, you have an opportunity to live your dharma, forging a joyful path through life that is yours and yours alone.

Creating a master financial plan helps you name some of your intentions and identify a path to pursue them. Usually, advisors will ask you about specific goals you're trying to reach as part of the planning process. But as you think about specific financial goals, don't lose sight of the real outcome you're trying to achieve: the ability to live your life as an authentic expression of your passionate being.

Before making any decisions about money targets or investments, I encourage clients to reflect deeply on how they want to move forward in this life. Take an apparently simple question—like, "How much money do you need in retirement?"—to find the answer, you first have to ask yourself a more fundamental question: "What do I want to do in retirement?" And to answer that question, you have to dig even deeper, exploring questions like: "What am I passionate about? What brings me fulfillment?" And ... the question I brought up a few chapters ago: "What brings me joy?"

Conducting this personal inventory allows you to move toward financial goals that align with your most authentic self. Too often, people set goals based on what they see their friends, family, neighbors, and colleagues doing, something I've mentioned already in this book. They decide they want to retire at 62 and own a particular type of car and a house in a desirable neighborhood. They send their children to the "right" schools, so they can get the "right" jobs. What they don't realize is that their friends, family, neighbors, and colleagues have likely formed their goals based on what they perceive their friends, family, neighbors, and colleagues want. The result is an echo chamber of inauthentic desires, which translate over time into inauthentic lives, and ultimately a whole lot of frustration and pain.

So, I encourage you to set goals that are truly your own. That's why when I created my own firm, we didn't establish financial goals until after undertaking the personal discovery sessions I described earlier. You must have that self-knowledge in place before you and your advisor can map out a vision of your financial future.

Another practice I recommend for authentic goal setting is to identify a range of desired outcomes, rather than pinning your hopes and future happiness on a specific date, number, or achievement. When I work with clients, I ask people first to dream big about their financial milestones—what are the ideal numbers for any key goal in your financial plan given all you know about yourself and your current situation? This doesn't mean simply naming the highest numbers you can think of; it means projecting high-end intentions that still seem achievable given your specific circumstances and expectations.

Take one of the goals that helps shape your overall financial plan: your desired retirement age. I suggest you think about the youngest age at which you'd like to retire. There's no right or wrong answer. Some people dream of living a life fully devoted to their hobbies. They want to sail around the world or build hang gliders or see as many species of birds as possible—for them, the ideal retirement age may be 55. Others are already living out their passions through their work and want to continue performing surgery or raising horses or developing code until they're in their seventies. The answer, as with all these questions, depends on who you are and what you're most passionate about.

You should put the same thought into another critical financial goal: how much money you need, after taxes, to support your lifestyle costs. This assessment is a little more complex because it includes potential expenses that range from mortgages and entertainment spending to how often you envision remodeling your home and buying a new car. It's important to be as thorough as possible when coming up with your ideal figure here. How much do you expect to pay for your kids' college educations? Do you want to take an annual vacation? If so, at what age do you see that coming to an end? Are you expected to take care of your parents or other family members? What kinds of insurance do you want? Behind each of these questions is a unique perspective and philosophy, and it's important to stay true to your vision. For example, you may be very wealthy but still want your children to pay for their own education, to ensure they have a stake in it. The key, again, is authenticity. What other people are doing with their money should have no bearing on what you do with yours.

Finally, don't overlook the importance of legacy goals, which include not only what you hope to leave for your children and grandchildren (and maybe nephews, nieces, or other family members) but what you dream of leaving to hospitals, universities, museums, churches, or other institutions. This is your opportunity to leave a mark on a part of the world that has made a difference in your life. And you don't have to wait until the end of your life— you can start right now.

One especially gratifying way to be benevolent with your wealth while you're still alive is through establishing a donor advised fund in the name of your family. You can make tax deductible contributions to these accounts with cash or highly appreciated assets, thus also avoiding capital gains taxes on those assets. You may also maintain control over how these gifts will be financially managed as they potentially grow tax free over the years in the investment markets.

Many of my clients have an annual family meeting—often centered around a holiday, like Thanksgiving—to discuss which charities they'd like their foundation to support over the next year. Beyond instilling lessons of benevolence, this also makes a natural forum for teaching lessons of money management. Discussing where the family foundation's money is managed and reviewing results provides invaluable lessons for the next generation. Involving the whole family in this way becomes a joyful celebration of giving and learning and can bring together family members across generations.

Once you've dreamed big and gotten inspired to imagine your ideal life, you should go back through your financial goals and decide what would be acceptable numbers in each of the categories. If you can't retire at 55, what about 60? What about 62? How much retirement income could you comfortably live on, even if you weren't bringing in as much as you hoped to in an ideal world? Would you be okay with a house within walking distance of the ocean instead of one with an ocean view? How about five weeks of travel instead of ten? By naming what's ideal and what's acceptable, you establish the bookends of your desired lifestyle.

Or think of it this way: Your ideal answers are the bullseye on a dartboard, and your acceptable answers are the dartboard's outer circle. Beyond the dartboard is the world of stress and confusion. I've read that 90% of all chronic diseases are caused by stress. By hitting somewhere on the board, you're setting yourself up for a good chance to avoid this stress. You're promoting a healthy body and mind. Maybe you'll hit the bullseye—some people do. Maybe you'll hit outside of the bullseye but away from the edges—that's the case with the majority of the clients I've worked with over the years. The most important result is that you're on the dartboard. In other words, you're within the parameters you've established by setting a range of ideal and acceptable goals. Knowing this range allows you to enter into a financial plan with confidence that you'll be secure, come what may.

Authentic goals are the foundation of a solid financial plan, but there's still plenty of work to do to set you on a course to achieve them. I learned over the years that many people—and even many advisors—think that the most important decision is to choose the right portfolio allocations to achieve your goals, as if an investment portfolio is synonymous with a financial plan. And, yes, it's easy to fixate on investment performance as if that and that alone determines your well-being, financial and otherwise. But while portfolio performance is important, it's not the most important determinant in meeting your goals—that honor belongs to your budget. For example, would you rather save a little less now, so you can support a more expensive lifestyle today, or save more, so you can meet bigger goals down the line? How much money are you able and willing to set aside each year to help you meet your projected retirement expenses and legacy goals?

In fact, a good financial plan has to consider many different variables that can affect your wealth and happiness. There are personal and family dynamics to understand, and deeper values that advisors must understand and respect. There is a wide range of interconnected financial variables beyond income, savings, and investments—such as insurance, real estate, taxes, and estate planning. With so many potential levers to pull to craft a plan that aligns with your personal vision, you need an advisory relationship that is fully committed to collaborating with you to create something greater than either side could create on its own.

That's why I was inspired to create a different kind of advisory firm when I launched Timonier in 1997. I recognized that true wealth management touches on multiple subjects that required specialized expertise, which led me to the family office model. For decades, the super-wealthy have enjoyed the benefits of working with an integrated diverse group of professionals who oversee all of their family's financial needs. That means wealth managers, accountants, tax specialists, attorneys, real estate advisors, and even risk managers are all coordinating from one office and serving that family's interests. I saw an opportunity to assemble a similar team and provide the same experience for my clients.

Many firms advertise that they "coordinate" with other professionals, like lawyers and accountants, for a holistic client experience. That's better than nothing, but it still results in a fragmented network in which clients have to go back and forth between all the people on their "team," trying to make sure everyone's more or less on the same page. Sadly, in most cases this sort of ad-hoc network doesn't function as a team at all. Even if they're in communication, it's likely that your accountant and your attorney won't have as complete an understanding of your financial outlook and life aspirations as your financial advisor (and that's assuming your advisor has done their due diligence, which, as we've seen, often isn't the case). Even in the best cases, misunderstandings and other failures of communication inevitably arise. In the worst cases, these professionals end up working at cross purposes, creating friction on your financial journey rather than clearing the path.

My vision was to create more than just a group of diverse professionals. I wanted a coherent unit bonded by mutual trust and working toward a common goal. Think of the crew of a ship. The captain can't steer the ship without the input of his shipmates, warning him of choppy waters or weather events ahead. The crew helps keep this ship in order and functioning properly—if it springs a leak, all hands are on deck to patch it up. Throughout the journey, all crew members are in constant communication with each other, keeping in mind their only goal: to sail from harbor of origin to harbor of destiny. But for my crew, our goal was to guide clients safely to the lifestyle they envisioned.

I've found there's incredible value in the formative act of bringing together multiple minds from different professional disciplines to ensure that each component of a client's plan is as strong as it can be. But whatever financial partners you work with, it's essential that they fully understand why you've established your lifetime goals and how they represent your deepest passions. That level of care and concern helps ensure you've found partners who are motivated to help you achieve the life you envision.

Of course, the circumstances of your life and finances will change over time. In response, a good financial plan should be fluid enough to incorporate these changes without risking your long-term wealth and well-being. Starting with authentic and inspired goals provides a touchstone for future adjustments to your plan, but the quality of your relationship with your financial advisor is also paramount. You should expect complete transparency between you and your financial partners. They have to be clear with you on every action they take and why they're taking it. Your responsibility is to share the important financial or emotional details that can help them keep you on course. That's why you and your financial advisor should review your master financial plan at least every year—and certainly after any major financial or lifestyle change that could affect your long-term outcome. During these reviews, you want to see that your advisor is comparing your investment performance against appropriate benchmarks while also updating you on the progress you're making toward lifetime goals. The intention of hitting the bullseye on the dartboard of your desired lifestyle should become a mantra.

That said, once you've put a plan in place, I urge you to "intend and detach." What I mean by this is to loosen the grip on your lifetime goals as you go about your day-to-day life. Those goals aren't going anywhere and fixating on the future (and how far you have to travel) takes you out of the moment you're living in right now. The creeping stress about a perceived lack of progress toward a certain goal, or an unexpected change in your circumstances, can cause you to miss other, fruitful pathways before you.

I encourage you to let your intentions hum underneath the current of your life—to let them guide you gently through your actions as you decide how much time you want to spend working, hanging out with your friends and family, pursuing hobbies, traveling the world, or whatever it is you most want to do today, and tomorrow, and the day after. The space between your intentions and your reality is a space of infinite possibility.

One practical way to incorporate your goals into the fabric of your life is to draft a "family mission statement." Bring all your family members together to talk about how you view yourselves and how you want to develop relationships, both inside and outside of the household. You might talk about how only positive choices, and not negative choices, will be supported. You might make it a goal to have an annual family gathering. You might mention spirituality. Financial matters might come into play, but they don't have to—a family mission statement is an opportunity to lay out what matters most to your family and to let those values guide you through life. It may be an opportunity to establish a different set of patterns for you and your children than the patterns that informed your early life. If you come from a story you aren't happy with, you can change that story for yourself and for the next generation. Many of my clients type out their statement and display it in their house so they can refer back to it again and again.

Meanwhile, with the right financial advisory team, you can be sure you have partners that are passionately focused on the performance of your plan as it relates to your lifetime journey—not the daily, weekly, or monthly fluctuations of the stock market or headline news.

You've probably seen how easy it is to get caught up in the roller coaster of rising and falling stock prices. As already noted, the Media is obsessed with following every twist and turn of this wild ride, and our lizard brains predispose us to react to market dips with fear and self-defense. But it is possible to detach from these primal emotions and trust in the long-term upward curve of global Capitalism. Remember, the assets in your investment portfolios—the assets that will help you move toward your goals and live your life to its fullest—aren't the abstract numbers we so often think of them as. In fact, they are shares of real companies working to overcome challenges and make life better for as many people around the globe as possible.

Which brings us back to your investment portfolio, which I've already said is not the most important factor in determining your financial future. Still, you're probably wondering how to choose which assets to include in your portfolio from among the hundreds of thousands available in the complex global marketplace. This task, like the rest of my ideal wealth management process, involves shedding our egos and seeing the world objectively, without judgments or biases. You don't need to hit investment grand slams or cut tax corners hiding your assets from Uncle Sam in Irish leasing companies to achieve your most lofty goals. In fact, what I've witnessed in my career, trying to do so puts your financial plans in jeopardy. You simply need to put an actionable plan in place to realize the results of what Capitalism provides. There's a method I've used for decades that helps my team wade through the chaotic and emotion-filled world of global markets. It's called "evidence-based investing."

CHAPTER 7 LUMINOUS INSIGHTS

We co-create a Master Financial Plan with our clients as a guidepost for their financial life journey. There are many aspects of life that we are not in control of, but there is so much that is within our control. The families that I worked with during my career are in control of four out of five of the major levers in accomplishing their financial goals: when they decide to retire, how much money they will save during their working years, how much money they will spend in retirement, and how much of a legacy they wish to leave to family members and charitable interests. They are not in control of the return on their investment portfolio. Not even the most conservative portfolio. But we can stress test these returns for the worst possible outcomes that have been experienced with our historical returns.

Achieving our most lofty goals, even with subpar investment results, will ideally hit the bullseye on a dartboard. If we've established goals that are too lofty to achieve, we still would like to know that we will enjoy a life and lifestyle that feels fulfilling and quite "acceptable." Our master financial plan will illustrate these results as hitting the dartboard but on the outer edges. The most impactful feedback of this detailed work is being able to illustrate that our clients are on track to hit the board. Not hitting the board indicates that our financial goals and journey of fulfillment are in jeopardy. Be in control and develop a healthy, loving relationship with your currency. The life-planning process has become so valuable to some families that they feel inspired to crown their work with a family mission statement. It incorporates all of their heartfelt values and rituals expressed in a single-page letter displayed prominently in their home as a reminder to all, what they hold sacred. You may want to create one as well.

CONTEMPLATIONS

- Make a list of the major aspects of your life (financial and non-financial) that you feel in control of and those things you don't feel in control of.
- Can some of the items you listed as uncontrollable be controlled? If for instance, you listed being stressed as uncontrollable, I would suggest you have the ability to change that category.
- Just as your biography writes the story of your biology, your lifestyle today writes the story of your future self. Work with your wealth advisory team and use the financial planning variables to test the possibilities of what you can create for yourself and family. This is how you bring dreams into reality.
- Spend some time writing a family mission statement. It doesn't have to be elaborate or lengthy and can be revised as you embrace its value.

CHAPTER 8

A MORE INTELLIGENT WAY: EVIDENCE-BASED INVESTING

Self-control is strength, calmness is mastery. You have to get to a point where your mood doesn't shift based on the insignificant actions of someone else. Don't allow others to control the direction of your life. Don't allow your emotions to overpower your conscious intelligence.

—MARCUS AURELIUS, PHILOSOPHER

WHEN I STARTED MY FIRM, I decided to do something that wasn't standard practice for most advisors, and certainly not something that bankers, investment brokers, or insurance brokers even considered. I would articulate in writing a wealth management philosophy. It would be a formal statement of process that I had been informally practicing for years. I knew I would need to formulate this to help my clients avoid succumbing to their lizard-brain fears and harmful, unconscious habits. Laying down a set of investment guidelines rooted in universal principles, I thought, could help counteract toxic biological and cultural conditioning—the conditioning that leads people to make decisions that hurt their finances and keep them from leading lives of true fulfillment. I also wanted the families considering our services to know that we were not following Financial Street's model, a system that had been hijacked by people who had lost all sense of integrity and morality in their dealings with those they were called to serve.

95

I wanted my investment philosophy to embody a new perspective, one that harnessed the power of owning companies to help families bring into being the lives they aspired to live. A big part of this new perspective was reframing the concept of risk. We've been conditioned to believe that the daily ups and downs of the markets represent a risk to all investors. Those ups and downs speak to the inevitable volatility that all markets undergo, but they have little to do with risk. In reality, the fundamental investment risk is not losing your money, but outliving it. This risk is especially potent as life expectancies increase and inflation erodes the value of your money. Many people these days are looking at upwards of 30 years of retirement. In those 30 years they should expect consumer prices to triple. So the big risk isn't temporary declines in your portfolio, it's the loss of your purchasing power as you grow older.

From this perspective, you start to see the flaws in the conventional wisdom about investing. You've probably heard of the popular guideline known as the "60/40 rule," which holds that investors should put 60% of their portfolio in stocks and 40% in bonds. Other rules of thumb swing even further toward bonds, with one adage dictating that the percentage of your portfolio held in bonds should be equal to your age—60% if you're 60, 70% if you're 70, etc. The purported goal of these strategies is to reduce volatility, but in reality they often are overly—even harmfully—conservative. They're designed to soothe those unconscious fears that so often emerge in response to even the slightest temporary decline in investment portfolio values.

Considering the true investing risk—the risk of outliving your money—the evidence suggests that stocks are much safer than people tend to assume. Since 1926, the average annual return for US stocks has been about 10%, compared to an inflation rate of about 3%. Temporary price declines, sometimes dramatic, do occur, but in time they're more than counterbalanced by the continuous long-term upward trend of stocks—a trend connected to a capital markets system that drives innovation, participation, and growth. Since 1926, there have only been 25 years that resulted in an overall price decline for major stocks. The odds of achieving positive returns are even better over longer holding periods. Of all the five-year rolling time periods since 1926, only 12 have resulted in declines.

Take another step back and the picture is even clearer. Of 15-year rolling time periods since 1926, none have resulted in a *decline*. Taking this research deep into left field, the rolling 30-year *volatility* of stocks is less than that of bonds relative to their respective returns. Said another way, the fluctuations of rolling 30-year returns for stocks is less than the fluctuations of rolling 30-year returns for bonds. Looking at this perspective statistically, stocks have averaged returns of 11.1% with a 1.3% standard deviation while bonds have averaged returns of 5.6% with a 2.7% standard deviation. Why isn't this information prevalent in the Media and Financial Street? Because they need your money in motion. And money in motion means profits for Financial Street—plus it sells newspapers and TV ads.

The key to investing successfully is in taking a LIFETIME perspective. My long-time colleague Nick Murray used to say, "No panic, no sell; no sell, no lose." Stock markets don't rise in a perfectly straight line, and it's likely that the inevitable temporary downturns will trigger your fight-or-flight response. But when you're following the proper wealth management philosophy, you can ride out these periods and benefit greatly from their long-term upward trajectory. That's why my philosophy embraces "*volatility* allowance," instead of "*risk* tolerance."

All investors must allow for the inevitable volatility of the markets. Some may have a slightly higher allowance than others—that's fine. The important thing is to recognize that volatility is inevitable and identify how much volatility you're willing to allow. Then we can create a diversified portfolio to reflect your preferences and hold to it (with adjustments as necessary) for your lifetime. Of course, the portfolio allocation must match the return needs of your master financial plan. If not, you need to have deeper discussions around emotional influences and behavior.

As a disciplined advisor, I don't sell investments during meaningful stock price declines. In fact, I am likely to be aggressively buying in these windows of time. As Baron Rothschild, an 18th-century British nobleman and member of the Rothschild banking family, is credited with saying, "The time to buy is when there's blood in the streets." He should know. Rothschild made a fortune buying in the stock market panic that followed the Battle of Waterloo against Napoleon. It all comes down to allying your energy with the undeniable force of global Capitalism.

But what about the more granular level of investing? When I was starting my firm, it was one thing to say I wanted to rely on the "power of markets" to grow my clients' wealth. But how would I decide which type of stocks to buy, when to buy them, and when to sell? What principles would guide my decisions? How could I be sure I was harnessing the full power of the markets and giving my clients the best possible chance of reaching their financial goals?

I was already well versed in the history of global markets, and, like many financial professionals, I was a proponent of Modern Portfolio Theory—the idea, developed in the early 1950s by Harry Markowitz, who received a Nobel Prize in Economics in 1990. It concluded that you can diversify portfolios to get the highest possible return at your desired level of volatility. The major asset classes used in this research were stocks, bonds, real estate, and treasury bills. Each asset class component was diversified with hundreds of individual securities. It further stated that 96% of a portfolio's return could be explained by the unique combinations of these asset classes. The other 4% of a portfolio's return was influenced by a manager's stock selections, market timing strategy, or the inclusion of other asset classes. Interestingly, these factors had a negative impact on a portfolio's returns. Now I deepened my analysis to provide current context to the research, with the goal of updating and improving my investment portfolio structures and processes.

One name that came up again and again was Eugene Fama, an economist at the University of Chicago School of Business. He's the ninth-most influential economist of all time, according to the Research Papers in Economics project, but most investors had never heard of him at the time of my research. Since then, he has shared in winning the 2013 Nobel Prize in Economic Sciences with Robert Shiller and Lars Peter Hansen. Fama rose to prominence in the 1960s when he developed something called the "efficient market hypothesis." Basically, this hypothesis says that financial markets process information almost instantaneously. When some new piece of news or data comes out that might affect the value of a company's stocks or bonds, the market incorporates that information into the price of those assets practically immediately.

What's so groundbreaking about this insight? It means that it's almost impossible for any investor to find a publicly traded security that's truly overvalued or undervalued. And that means that the dominant paradigm of investing is based on the false assumption that you can outwit the markets by spotting a potential "winner" that no one else has seen, or by betting on so-called undervalued assets.

Fama's efficient market hypothesis resonated with my experience. I'd spent decades watching fellow financial pros try to pick stocks and time the market's movements to gain an edge—a strategy called "active investing." Active managers claim to have enough intellectual skills to consistently outperform their respective market benchmarks with their economic forecasts and stock selection prowess. Their strategies pay off occasionally, but over the long term, they lose to their assigned benchmarks more often than they win. It was something I'd seen over and over again. I even wrote down by hand in a chart the returns of well over 200 stock, bond, and real estate portfolio managers along with their index benchmarks every quarter for 18 years, as these findings became self-evident. I gained a great understanding of managers and markets by this meditative exercise.

There's a mountain of evidence to back up my observations. A Morningstar report for the 20-year period ending on December 31, 2022, found that only 17% of all active US-domiciled stock funds outperformed their respective benchmarks. Of the original funds that were tracked, only 44% were in business after this 20-year period. We will return to alternate investment strategies in a moment but know that dozens of other studies have shown similar results. To emphasize this point, independent investment management research organizations such as Dalbar, Inc. and Morningstar, Inc. year in and year out consistently draw the same conclusions about the results of active management. Their databases include metrics on over 621,000 stocks, mutual funds, and other investment products around the globe. Their major conclusions:

1. The vast majority of active fund managers underperform their stock and bond market benchmarks over rolling intermediate-term and long-term timeframes. Their

statistics become materially worse when you compare their after-tax results to these benchmarks.

2. Fund managers in aggregate are incapable of outperforming with market timing strategies (selling out before market declines and buying back in at market bottoms). Again, for taxable investors, this strategy's underperformance widens when looking at after-tax returns.

3. Mutual fund investors and investment management consultants are ill-advised to invest based on prior active fund manager performance. Looking at the top quartile managers for the prior three, five, and ten years is not a predictor for repeating their results.

All the evidence points in the same direction: Over the long term, and in spite of massive organizations, time spent on research and intellectual talent from prestigious universities, active managers guess wrong more often than they guess right in their attempt to outperform their unmanaged benchmarks. And yet the majority of advisors still follow the active investing model. Why? Because it's not the professionals who are losing out. It's their investors. These advisors continue to collect fees from all their buying and selling strategies while their clients' returns suffer. They even use deceptive techniques to eliminate their histories of poor performance while retaining their asset management fees. Banks, investment institutions, mutual fund companies, and insurance companies do this by merging an underperforming fund in their lineup into a better performing fund they are also managing, sometimes even collecting a higher compensation. In doing this, the track record of the poor performing fund vanishes into thin air. I've personally witnessed this countless times during my career.

I knew I didn't want to participate in that all-too-pervasive practice, and Fama's efficient market hypothesis gave me solid ground to stand on. My wealth management work required investment strategies that would provide continuity of results over my clients' lifetimes and beyond. But while the mountain of evidence demonstrated how not to invest, it didn't solve the problem of how to invest—and what, exactly, to invest in.

Index funds offer one alternative. As their name suggests, index funds invest in the stocks and bonds that make up a particular market segment. The most famous index fund, the Vanguard 500 Index, mirrors holdings of the market cap-weighted S&P 500 index of companies in the United States. When this index goes up, investors win—and historically, given a long enough time frame, the S&P 500 has always had positive returns. Index funds avoid the risk of poor market timing and making bad bets by simply holding without trading a wide sample of stocks for as long as they remain in the index. Because there are all kinds of market indexes, investors can create a diversified portfolio of several index funds that span various asset classes worldwide. What's more, these funds come with much lower management fees than active funds, putting even more money in the investor's pocket. To top it off, if you are a taxable investor, due to a lower turnover of the portfolio, these funds have a higher after-tax result than their active manager counterparts. What's not to love?

A couple of things. First, since true index funds must hold exactly the same stocks as their underlying indexes, these funds are forced to buy and sell stocks when the once-a-year composition of the index changes, often resulting in negative tax consequences for investors. These taxable distributions are less than what the active managers are producing, but they produce taxation nonetheless. Second, and more consequentially, index funds fail to identify segments within their market baskets that may deliver better returns than others. They're solid investment vehicles, and they're almost always a better option than actively managed funds, but it's important to note that they leave a lot of money on the table. Index funds will always lose to the performance of their respective stock and bond benchmarks but only by the thinnest of margins caused by their typically low fees to assemble and administer to these accounts.

What I discovered as I dug deeper into academic investment research is that there's a middle ground between actively managed mutual funds and market-mimicking managed index funds. It was Eugene Fama, along with fellow economist Kenneth French, who did the most to carve out this space. In the 1990s, Fama and French conducted research that aimed to identify what exactly drove stock returns. Their thinking was that if high-performing equities shared certain characteristics, investors could tilt their portfolios toward particular types of stocks and capture better returns than broader allocations of index funds. This strategy would allow investors to pursue the classic goal of "beating the market," without the costly and ultimately futile effort of trying to select individual stocks and time the market's ups and downs. No forecasting was needed.

Fama and French identified three main attributes—which they called "factors"—that drive expected returns: *market risk*, *size*, and *value*. This three-factor asset pricing model provided a blueprint for how to invest in a way that maximized returns and minimized *volatility*. This blueprint, because it's based on the weighty evidence provided by analysis of long-term historical market data, is how evidence-based investing got its name. And, the more in-depth research I conducted along with my own experiential years in managing money, the more I knew it would be the approach I took in constructing customized portfolios based on my clients' goals.

To better understand how evidence-based investing works, let's take a closer look at the three factors singled out by Fama and French. The first factor, *market risk*, reflects the data I've covered already: Over time, stocks have a higher return than US treasury bills. Stocks are more volatile than treasury bills—meaning their prices can rise and fall more dramatically in short periods—but over time they deliver higher returns.

The second factor is *size*. What Fama and French showed (and what other research has backed up since) is that stocks of smaller companies, as a whole, outperform the stocks of larger companies over time.

The third factor, *value*, is based on the premise that paying less for a set of future cash flows is associated with a higher expected return. That's one of the most fundamental tenets of investing. Fundamentally, these companies have low price-to-book ratios as well as low price-to-earnings ratios. *Value* stocks typically have a bargain price as investors see the company as unfavorable in the marketplace. No matter investor perception, data covering nearly a century in the US, and over 50 years of data outside the US, supports the observation that stocks with lower relative prices outperform those with higher relative prices. The only exception to this rule is Italy.

All the historical evidence available supports the claim that these three factors—*market risk*, *size*, and *value*—capture higher returns repeatedly through rolling windows of time, which is a reason why the factors are also called "premiums." Historically, they've given you a premium over the broader market's return. But why? The answer, again, has to do with risk. Individual stocks are riskier than individual bonds, individual small-cap stocks are riskier than individual large-cap stocks, and individual *value* stocks are riskier than individual growth stocks. As usual when it comes to risk, the potential reward for taking on this *risk* is higher than the potential reward for less risky investments.

But the real insight of evidence-based investing is that when you invest in a broad array of stocks with the above-mentioned three factors, you can manage that risk very effectively. That's because if a handful of your companies perform badly—or even if one of the factors underperforms for a short period (as they sometimes do)—those declines may be counterbalanced by the long-term positive performance of the other companies and factors in your portfolio. Thus, risk is replaced by the management of volatility—a very different landscape indeed. As mentioned above, the weighty evidence shows that over time, and as a group, stocks beat bonds; the same goes for small-cap stocks versus large-cap stocks, and for *value* stocks versus growth stocks.

More recently, a body of research has injected a fourth factor into the mix: *profitability*. So now I'd add: Over time, and as a group, stocks from companies with higher *profitability* beat stocks from companies with lower *profitability*. While any one of these factors can lag for a time, they have always come back stronger than the broad market.

This is the formula, at its most basic, for evidence-based investing, and it's what I adopted as my investment philosophy when I started my firm more than a quarter of a century ago. Dimensional Fund Advisors, Vanguard, and later Avantis Investors were the fund companies that I partnered with to build our portfolio strategies. I relied on Dimensional for the vast majority of the work. Dimensional is not a household name, and, in fact, most of the Financial Street investment community has not heard of Dimensional. There are two main reasons for this. One, they don't advertise. I refer to them as the clean room at NASA. They are the most client-centric organization through and through that I've ever witnessed and been associated with. And keeping costs down is a primary attribute. They consistently rank in the top one percentile for lowest fees for managing assets in the entire industry. And two, a registered investment advisor and their firm must go through a vigorous approval process to access Dimensional's mutual funds and resources. The prerequisites involve educational courses and submitting statements of philosophy that an advisor will adhere to. If someone is with a Financial Street firm that charges commissions, you won't be considered.

Founded in 1981, and now with over 1,500 employees in 14 global offices, Dimensional manages over $615 billion in assets as of March 31, 2023. They have five Nobel Prize laureates in economics as directors strategically affiliated with them. Additionally, the University of Chicago Booth School of Business is named after Dimensional co-founder David Booth. Many of the greatest advancements in finance have come from their academic research. Dimensional is a pioneer in bringing those discoveries to the markets.

So, as we did with understanding whether or not active management could outperform an index strategy, how has Dimensional fared? A Morningstar report for the 20-year period ending on December 31, 2022, found that 79% of all their US-domiciled stock funds outperformed their respective benchmarks. Additionally, of the original funds that were tracked in this study, all were still in existence after this 20-year period. None was closed or merged into other funds. I feel fortunate to have discovered Dimensional when I began my firm and feel equally blessed after such a long relationship and experience with them. Continuity of results is critical in the management of family wealth. And, they have proven their unique value time and again.

Like life itself, our philosophies are subject to evolution, so I stay apprised of new research and studies and continue to test this investing methodology. But the core of this approach remains the same: You can attain your lifetime goals through detailed financial planning that relies on returns of the global marketplace. You don't need to take bets on markets or a single security, and you don't need to avail yourself of high-risk tax strategies to avoid the IRS. With an evidence-based approach, you get all of the available return from the marketplace—no more, because there is no more, and no less.

Diversification is an inherent aspect of evidence-based investing, and extreme diversification is a hallmark of the investing approach I espouse for clients. By structuring global portfolios with tilts toward the factors I've just mentioned, you can avoid the unsystematic risk of owning a few individual companies— because even some of the largest and oldest companies go out of business. Remember WorldCom, Lehman Brothers, Wachovia, Bear Stearns, Enron, Compaq, Pan Am, Thornburg Mortgage? They don't exist anymore. With an evidence-based portfolio that my firm designed, General Electric could go bankrupt, and as you sipped your morning coffee, you would simply say, "Pass me the almond milk please." That's because your portfolio would hold more than 10,000 companies in the US and around the world, including stocks in emerging market countries. It would avoid directly investing in assets that are popular in some circles, like gold, whose long-term return is about the same as the rate of inflation with the volatility of small-cap stocks. Instead, it would feature a mix of asset classes that are non-correlated—that is, assets whose prices don't all move in the same direction or at the same magnitude at the same time. That way, when one set of assets is affected by market forces, another set may be entirely unaffected, or even move in the opposite direction. It all comes back to leveraging and balancing the volatility in individual assets to create a diversified portfolio that works to your lifetime benefit.

Even with an evidence-based approach, I continually fine-tune individual client portfolios based on their specific goals. But the big difference between this approach and other investors' is that you're not at risk of letting emotions guide your decisions. You can be sure you're not chasing the latest "hot" stock or having your funds constantly switched based on the past year's performance or even the past five years' performance. And when the markets decline dramatically—like they did in March 2020 during the coronavirus pandemic—you're protected from panic-selling any assets that are negatively affected. In fact, after the stock markets breached a 30% decline in 2020, all we did was begin rebalancing our client portfolios to take advantage of those declines and cheaper company prices. Bond prices had held steady, and we were in general buying more stock positions by selling some bond assets.

In general, when stock prices fall temporarily during a client's working years, I view that as a chance to buy even more shares than their savings were able to buy before. But the investment approach we developed at my firm allows clients to stay unphased even when stock prices fall during their retirement years—because we created processes to navigate temporary market declines in advance. Most of my firm's clients fit into one of two retiree financial profiles. One group is families who have been so frugal with their savings, relative to the cost of their lifestyle, and confident in the capital market system with their investment holdings that they can live on their social security and pension income benefits supplemented by dividends and interest income of their globally diversified investment portfolios. While stock prices will dip and even plummet temporarily from time to time, dividends are very reliable and consistent in their payouts. Research from the NYU Stern School of Business shows that dividends from the S&P 500 US companies have more than doubled in value every ten years since 1960, far outpacing the rate of inflation. They have only declined year-over-year on two occasions during those six decades.

Thanks to dividend income, this group of clients can just yawn when stock prices decline. For example, the global stock market declined 20% in the fourth quarter of 2018. Financial Street was promoting panic even though we'd seen a 20% gain in corporate earnings for the year. But our clients living on dividend income benefitted from an 8% year-over-year increase in these payouts. They could not have cared less what the short-term market prices were saying.

In order to meet their lifestyle goals, most people, however, need more income than they get from their stock dividends and bond interest payments. For these clients, we systematically sell shares in their stock holdings to supplement their income needs. I always make sure they have enough holdings in cash and short-maturity bonds to cover at least two to three years of income needs. This represents a period of time longer than almost all historical market declines, and I call it the Cash Reserve Strategy. I never want clients to have to sell stock positions that have experienced a material price decline in order to produce an income stream.

Instead, when markets decline—as they will do periodically—we can sell cash equivalents and bond positions to produce the income clients need. Then, as the markets regain equilibrium, it's easy to shift back to selling stock and real estate shares to supplement their dividend and interest income to produce a desired level of income. Thus, we, not the market, remain in control. And clients can sleep well, knowing that market fluctuations will not affect their cash flow or impact the integrity of their stock and real estate holdings over time.

Discipline is the key to maintaining an evidence-based, lifetime investing approach. Once we've developed the right portfolio for each client based on their goals and allowance for volatility, we keep it in line by regularly rebalancing among our chosen assets. Inevitably, some investments in your portfolio will outperform others, causing an imbalance of our targeted weightings. When these imbalances exceed a certain percentage, we rebalance the portfolio. So, in essence, we are always methodically paring down over time from the assets that have enjoyed excess returns and adding to those assets that cyclically underperformed. It is a forced version of buying low and selling high. No forecasting is needed.

We don't like to create a taxable event when we are managing taxable portfolios. So, we can typically rebalance a portfolio with new client contributions and dividends being produced in the account, buying only underweight assets to bring them back to target allocation. With tax deferred accounts, we can simply sell the assets above our targeted weightings and buy the underweighted assets because there are no tax consequences to the account. That way, we can help make sure that our portfolios retain the long-term consistency and return potential that we expect based on our carefully determined mix of investments.

Even with all of these moving parts, what I appreciate more than anything about evidence-based investing is its clarity and simplicity. This may strike some people as an odd connection, but when I discovered evidence-based investing more than 27 years ago, it resonated strongly with the discoveries I was beginning to make through my meditation practice. Meditation was helping me to see the world objectively, as it really was, from a place of stillness. Evidence-based investing is all about objectivity and focusing on the facts and historical evidence—not projections or dramatic reactions—and it brought about a similar sense of peace, and even joy. I loved how it removed my own ego from my decision-making process and brought me in closer touch with reality.

Active management, which is still the predominant mode of investing on Financial Street, is full of egotism and fantasy. When active managers try to identify undervalued individual stocks that no one else has noticed or stocks with higher growth factors that others aren't seeing, not only do they assume they're somehow smarter than everyone else in the industry, but they also reject reality by turning a blind eye to the historical evidence about how the markets work. Evidence-based investing, on the other hand, keeps the focus squarely on what we know (what the evidence tells us about long-term asset performance) and what we can control (our portfolio allocations and the discipline to stay the course). My fulfillment as an advisor comes not from gaming the system but from wisely participating in the system and helping people realize their dreams.

I also see the satisfaction and serenity it helps bring to clients who've embraced evidence-based investing. On March 13, 2020, just a few weeks after panic selling in stocks from the onset of COVID-19, an 89-year-old client walked into our office and said he had had a relatively large CD mature at his bank and wanted to add to his emerging market value portfolio and his emerging market small company value portfolio. Though the CD was large, it was less than 1% of all his assets with us. Now, in retrospect, we had made the additions ten days before the stock market finally bottomed. They declined 20% more before the recovery began. He would periodically call to check on his additions but was never concerned, just curious of his intuitive senses. Almost 14 months later his additions easily made up for the temporary decline: they were up 58% and 72%, respectively, from his purchase price. For comparison, the S&P 500 Index was up 59% in the same timeframe. I'd say he was feeling pretty good about himself. Who says you have to buy bonds as you age?

This client isn't really investing for himself these days. He doesn't even spend all of the dividends from his stocks or interest from his bonds. He's investing for his children, his grandchildren, his great grandchildren, and his charitable interests. He is a very enlightened and beautiful man, having spent years of service as a physician. You could just see the inner joy and peace in him when he came through our office doors. He adopted our shareholder mantra, understands how Capitalism works, and through his light is expressing his own a-bun-dance. His outer securities are a reflection of his inner security.

That said, I always have some clients who come to me during market declines to ask me if our portfolio strategy is still working. In fact, there is always someone asking me this even when times are good. The answer has always been—yes. In the rarest of cases, a client has requested that we pull out of the stock markets anyway. When this happens, I remind them of our evidence-based buy-and-hold lifetime policy and the reasons for holding the course. With this professional review and a pause from their reactionary minds, they have all but in the rarest of occasions returned to a calm state of awareness. The few that haven't I asked to spend the necessary time, but they found another financial advisory relationship.

There has been one exception to this rule in my entire career. I believe that advisors are not in the business of being order takers. That's what brokers do. We are hired to advise, establish an agreed-upon lifetime plan, and be a guide to conscious choices. The one time I assented to a client's request to sell is a great example of why it never makes sense to cave in to your fears during times of market unrest.

I started working with Allison and her husband, Wayne, both anesthesiologists, after meeting Wayne on the golf course in 1985. Wayne was 20 years older than Allison. She was a fireball, full of emotion, always in an uproar about this or that. Wayne used to kid with me that he thought his first name was Dammit and his middle name was Wayne. I liked both of them immediately, and over time we became like family. They even took care of my mother's aunt for ten days, so my parents could celebrate their 50th wedding anniversary in Hawaii, having to drive a thousand miles to do so. There was a lot of love between us.

After Wayne died, Allison moved from Florida, where they'd retired, to Hendersonville, North Carolina, to be closer to her daughter, grandchildren, and siblings. One of those siblings was her older brother, John, who she admired as a young child. John had the dominant personality in the family as well. He'd started a business that developed stealth radio technology, and it was having a lot of success. But all his money was tied up in his business—he didn't have anything resembling an IRA and had a modest amount in a company 401(k) plan. When the market began sinking in 2008, he panicked and moved what investments he had into a gold fund. He also bought land in Georgia that had old military bunkers in case the apocalypse really came to fruition.

I wouldn't have known about any of this if Allison hadn't called me. She let me know that John had implored her to "get the hell out of the stock markets as soon as possible." It was March 5, 2009. She was in an absolute panic and full meltdown. I knew if her husband, Wayne, had been there, he would have absorbed all her emotions which would have given her the time and space needed to calm down. I tried to play that role, but she wasn't connecting with what I was saying from a long-distance phone call. She was adamant that we sell her IRA, the whole stock portfolio. Her brother had set off a fear reaction, and she was in full fight-or-flight mode. I tried every angle I could think of to reason with her conscious mind to ride out the storm. But her conscious mind had temporarily checked out.

I talked about historical market performance and the inevitability of temporary declines. I explained how negative emotions could give way to a more objective perspective, given a little bit of time. I talked about her account specifically. For over 25 years, it had been outperforming the global benchmarks by a wide margin, and she had experienced many market downturns in doing so. But she was adamant. She wasn't having any of what I was saying. She insisted I liquidate all securities and place the proceeds in a money market fund. And so ... I did. Without a doubt, from a wealth management perspective, this was the most tragic event in my career.

The very next day, March 6, was the day the stock markets were priced at their lowest point during the Great Financial Recession. Her desire to liquidate was perfectly wrong. Over the next several months, they rose steadily, and by September it was clear that they were back on the general upward trend. The Media terrorism and market noise had subsided.

On September 29, Allison called me up. She started by apologizing. She'd felt the fight-or-flight impulse, and she'd flown. She saw now it was a ginormous mistake. She said she was ready to take her money and put it back in the market, and that's what we did.

For my own understanding and analysis, I calculated what she'd missed out on by removing her money from the global stock market for those six months. The S&P 500 Index was up 50% in that window of time. US large company value stocks were up 74%, US small-cap stocks were up 85%, and US real estate was up 90%. Allison had 80% of her money in global stocks and real estate, and 20% in bonds. If she had not sold out her portfolio, she would have been rewarded with a 58% return. Looking at these numbers, I knew that I'd never again make the mistake of withdrawing a client's funds from the market, no matter how close they were to me or how vociferously they insisted. And I haven't.

Knowing how we are programmed from birth, I saw that Allison's actions were dictated by her subconscious conditioning. Without thinking, her mind and body were instinctively making choices based on the admired brother from childhood. It didn't matter that he had no experience with investment management. He made the sounding alert that a lion was near, and his panic became her panic.

My clients' portfolios do take hits from time to time, but in the long run, evidence-based investing has consistently delivered outcomes in line with their goals. Because this is the case, evidence-based investing takes emotion off the table for decision making. When you invest based on a proven philosophy, you can break the cycle of fear and regret that dominates most investors' emotional lives. You're not always looking for the next best thing. You can relax, think clearly, and focus your energy in a more positive and beneficial direction. You can ignore the stories circulated by Financial Street and the catastrophist Media—or your brother John—that make even a short-term market downturn seem like an apocalyptic event, stories that are tailored to bypass your conscious brain and head straight to your amygdala, producing fear and panic. Instead, you can start paying attention to your own story. The one, in the absence of wasted time and worry, you imagine and manifest from your authentic, heart-based aspirations. An unfolding story that all humankind seeks at the level of consciousness they individually are experiencing. Capitalism can support that journey to collective enlightenment and the vast creations that result from this harmony.

In the final view, we're investing not in the anonymous entities we call stocks or assets, but in the structure of global Capitalism itself. We are taking ownership by buying shares in thousands of the largest, most soundly financed, most profitable, and most innovative companies in the world. This system, imperfect as it is, is all about people coming together to solve problems and enhance the human experience. And if there's one thing I've learned over the course of my career, it's this: you never want to bet against human beings to solve known problems.

CHAPTER 8 LUMINOUS INSIGHTS

A key element to investing successfully is in taking not just a long-term outlook but, a lifetime perspective. When you invest based on a proven philosophy, you can break the cycle of fear and regret that dominates most investors' emotional lives. Rather than active strategies or index strategies, it is evidence-based investing strategies that have yielded the best results. Evidence-based investing strategies discovered four major factors, which large swaths of assets and companies embodied, consistently drove higher expected returns. They found that stocks consistently outperformed bonds, that small-sized companies outperformed large companies, that low-priced stocks outperformed high-priced stocks, and that high-profitability companies outperformed low-profitability companies. And no economic forecasting or market timing efforts were required to achieve these results.

The researchers and organization behind evidence-based investing was Dimensional Fund Advisors. Morningstar, Inc. found that 79% of Dimensional's US stock funds have outperformed their respective benchmarks through rolling 20-year time periods. The continuity of the results of these low tax cost funds are impressive.

CONTEMPLATIONS

- What is your or your portfolio manager's investment philosophy? Do they rely on economic forecasting for their portfolio decisions? Do they attempt to time their participation in the markets?
- Are your portfolios managed with active managers, index funds, evidence-based funds, individual stocks and bonds, hedge funds, private equity, or some other method?
- Have their performance records been tracked over rolling timeframes?
- Have you evaluated your family's total holdings against a custom benchmark reflecting your holdings asset class weightings?
- Is your investment portfolio matching the assumed returns used in your master financial plan?

CONCLUSION: CONNECTING WITH YOUR HIGHER SELF

We are travelers on a cosmic journey—stardust, swirling and dancing in the eddies and whirlpools of infinity. Life is eternal. But the expressions of life are ephemeral, momentary, transient.
—GAUTAMA BUDDHA

'VE SPENT A GOOD DEAL of my adult life on the path of self-discovery. That path has taken me from Winston-Salem, North Carolina, to Sydney, Australia, to Rhinebeck, New York, to La Jolla, California, to Chennai, India, to Guanacaste, Costa Rica, to Damanhur, Italy, and to Los Lobos, Chile. Each step in this journey has brought me a deeper understanding of myself and the world, but one of the most powerful experiences I have had occurred during that two-week tour of Indian temples I mentioned a few chapters ago. This was the trip I went on in 2006, just months after my daughter's passing.

I joined a group of 20 from the US and Europe, and the only activity of interest we had in common was that we all meditated. We visited six cities in the Tamil Nadu region of India, beginning in Chennai, moving to the former French colony of Pondicherry on the Bay of Bengal, then visiting the city of Swamimalai known for its provocative architecture, then Tiruvannamalai, home of southern India's largest temple, and finally culminating with a visit to the 2,500-year-old city of Madurai, referred to as the sleepless city of India.

Along the way we stopped and had dinner and a festive evening with the Prince of Tanjore at his palace, accompanied by a fire parade and entertained through dinner with veiled belly dancers.

115

We spent our days living in ashrams, visiting temples, listening to educational and spiritual lectures, experiencing the vast extremes of life, having sat sings with local gurus, and soaking in much time of contemplation and meditation.

During our stay in Tiruvannamalai, something I thought was set in stone—something so close to me and such a part of my identity that I couldn't imagine it ever changing—suddenly became something new: my name.

Our first day began with a 13-mile pilgrimage around Mt. Arunachala at dawn, as we witnessed the life of India waking in all of its color and gratitude, from rich to poor, from oxen-driven fields to mothers attending to their daughter's readiness for school in their hand-washed colorful uniforms. On day two, after waking at 4 a.m. to a cold shower, I meditated for two hours. I then walked across the street to the Sri Bhagavan Ramana Maharshi Ashram for breakfast, where we sat on the concrete floors of the dining hall with a banana leaf serving as our plate.

On the way, there were food carts on one side of the street and a group of Sadhus on the other side. Sadhus are men who have renounced materialism and are making their way by living solely on the gifts from the earth. It could be that one of them was an attorney who, at age 46, announced to his wife and six children that he wouldn't be coming home any longer. I make no judgments about this. But some of them in the early going need help to survive, and they find their way to an ashram in hope of some assistance. They are identified by wearing nothing but an orange robe. They weren't begging, but I went over to them and gave them some money for breakfast. As I turned and walked away, one of the Sadhus ran up to me and with his hands in prayer said, "Thank you. I name you Jai!"

"Jai?" I said.

"Yes," he said. "In Hindu 'jai' means 'victory.' And today is my victory. You gave me food to eat."

Then he spread holy ash on my forehead. He was about 5-foot 4, bald, and held a massive smile. I cherish the memory of sharing this moment with him that morning more than 17 years ago, halfway around the world.

Being benevolent, supporting our community with financial gifts or gifts of time and effort—this has always been a central aspect of my family. Sharing our bounty with others returns gifts in unexpected ways. One of mine is the name I now go by: Jai.

While it would be impossible to solicit my friends, clients, family, and colleagues to begin referring to me as Jai at this point in my long life, I now ask those I meet for the first time to please refer to me as Jai. It's light, it's a beautiful memory, it's positive, and it shows what happens when we recognize in each other that we are connected.

As I continue to attend gatherings with other seeking souls, people from all walks of life and from all corners of the world, I have a rule to never initiate a discussion by asking people what they do for a living. I prefer to connect with them on a deeper level before we get into the particulars of our careers. Eventually, though, someone usually asks me the question: "What do you do for a living?" When I tell people that I've spent most of my adult life in wealth management, they tend to react with disbelief. How can I be so spiritual, they wonder, and yet so bound up with money?

My response is always the same: "That tells me more about you than it does about me." As I have sought to convey in this book, money is neither good nor bad—it's simply a neutral tool. In this way, money is like nuclear power. You can use nuclear power to blow up a city, or you can use it to cool buildings and light up that city's homes. It's the character revealed through the use of the tool that makes it good or bad, not the tool itself. The responses I received after revealing my chosen career path told me that these people didn't have a good relationship with money. Of course, that just meant they were like the majority of people I've come across in my decades as a wealth manager, from recent college graduates to high-powered executives. Say the word "money," and the sensation you feel in your body will likely be negative, no matter your station in life.

By now, I hope you've absorbed the key message of this book— it doesn't have to be this way. You can develop a relationship with money that's aligned with your deepest values and that helps you walk a more conscious path through life. You get to choose how you relate to money, just as you get to choose how you relate to the people you interact with every day, the activities you engage in, and the attitude you bring to your work. You get to decide what matters to you. Once you know that, you can set an intention to live in a way that brings you meaning and fulfillment. You can choose not to associate with people who hinder you on your path toward realizing your dreams. You can choose to treat yourself and others with benevolence. You can choose to live your dharma. All it takes is an awakened awareness—and you can choose to be self-aware. Aware with the quality that expands beyond an object or an event and opens you to creative leaps and insights integrating all of life's possibilities, seen and unseen.

Of course, many things lie outside of your control. All investors must come to terms with inevitable but unpredictable market downturns, from run-of-the-mill daily blips to more dramatic recessions. In the course of my career, I've witnessed the 25% one-day plummet in the S&P 500 index on October 19, 1987; the market slump in response to the 1990 to 1991 Gulf War; the dot com bubble resulting in a two-year 78% decline of the NASDAQ index; and the Great Recession of 2008 and 2009 resulting in a US stock market collapse of more than 55% (our generation's Great Depression), among countless other market declines that lasted minutes (the May 2010 10% Flash Crash), days, weeks, or months. While writing this book, the COVID-19 pandemic created a global stock market decline of over 34%, and it spread across the world, causing severe economic disruption to the global economy.

Our brain processes these events through a built-in operating system that wasn't designed to respond to the cacophony of signals about market performance it receives every day. The human brain is wired for survival. When it senses a threat, it sends us into fight, flight, or freeze mode. This works well if we're being stalked by a lion, but it has disastrous consequences when making decisions about money. And the constant worry creates debilitating dis-ease in the body. None of our ancestors did anything remotely resembling the sort of investing that people are expected to do today. Our ancestors did not save. In fact, if they tried to save, they were viewed as hoarders and kicked out of the tribe.

It's only in the last 50 or 60 years—a blink of an eye in human history—that the majority of people in the developed world have been asked to take charge of their investments.

During those decades, a sophisticated and self-serving industry has emerged to take advantage of our reptilian brains. Financial Street professionals—aided by the Media and by our hypnotized neighbors and colleagues—tell stories and myths designed to stoke fear or greed. Their goal is to obscure the truth and manipulate us into moving our money from one investment product to another, one insurance product to another, so that the fees and commissions keep rolling their way. By knowing how our minds operate better than we do, we become the puppets and they are the puppeteers.

Neither the DNA we all share nor the attitudes and predilections we acquire from our environment have equipped us to deal with the volatility inherent in stock markets or the bad actors willing to exploit us. These obstacles to your financial and spiritual well-being aren't going away anytime soon. But once you know they're there, you can choose to transcend them.

You can choose to acknowledge the reality that market declines are always temporary, and the upward trend is permanent. (Starting in February of 2020, the market sank 34% in 33 days—and by August it had returned to all-time highs, despite the negative headline news.)

You can choose to cultivate self-awareness, exploring your subconscious mind to identify the beliefs that have shaped your current experience. Then you can choose to develop a new story around those beliefs that do not serve you, retaining the ones that do. You can choose to live an intentional life from your authentic desires, one that you are the master of.

You can choose to engage in habits and practices that allow you to observe the impulses of your mind without allowing them to dictate your actions. Meditation is the tool that has worked best for me over the years in fostering this sense of emotional intelligence. I'm finding in recent times that breathwork and qi gong have powerful parallel benefits for the health of the body and mind.

And you can choose not to operate within the corrupt system of Financial Street, and to ignore the Media that amplifies its voice. You can choose instead to partner with a fiduciary team that truly has your best interests in mind, one that operates from a position of transparency and non-judgment, and that takes into account each client's unique circumstances, attitudes, desires, and goals. A partner that takes the time to get to know you on a personal level, so they can provide the guidance designed to work for you and your family. A partner that will help you build and maintain a balanced and comfortable relationship with money. A relationship charged with positive energy. A partner that serves as a sanctuary, a safe haven for families to live out their dreams in collaboration with a multi-disciplinary professional team of advisors working on your behalf. A team rich in integrity and morality.

Here's a simple rule: If a financial professional is trying to convince you to do something—run. They may lay claim to the title of advisor, but they really are just salespeople. Learn to listen to your intuition—and don't confuse this with your gut, which is emotional. Listen to that tiny voice that whispers truth into your awareness. All too often, people ignore this aspect of themselves and later experience remorse for listening to the opinions of others. So, stop following the herd. This is your life!

Investing is a lifetime journey—and one that can actually extend beyond your life and carry over into future generations of your family and other beneficiaries. Short-term market timers and tactical asset movement strategists skip across the surface of the global economy and are always falling prey to the slightest headwind. Lifetime investors, on the other hand, tap into the deeper flow of global Capitalism. Investing with faith, patience, and purpose connects you with a worldwide network of companies that are constantly generating new ideas and inventions to make life better for human beings. This system of global Capitalism provides jobs and social experiences for those who participate in it, bringing together people representing myriad walks of life for the common good. It's helping to create a world in which more people are living more abundantly, in better health, and with longer lives, than ever before.

This form of conscious investing allows you to experience a fundamental truth about life on earth: We are all connected. We are more than skin-encapsulated bags of bones. We live in a material world, but we are multidimensional beings. As I write these words, there are approximately eight billion people in the world, and this number is expected to grow by about 2.5 billion in the next 30 years before leveling off. It's easy to go through life imagining that, with the few exceptions of your friends and family, you have little to do with these billions of people walking around on the same planet as you. It's easy to imagine that we're all separate entities. But beneath our physical, surface-level realities, we all partake of something eternal. We're all a part of the same universal light. When you live in acknowledgment of this truth, you can experience wealth in a form closer to its original meaning of abundance. I encourage you to take a step toward true wealth, whether it's your first step or the next of many you've already taken on your unique journey. You can choose to live in joy and abundance. I invite you to unveil your luminous light.

CONTEMPLATIONS

- Now that you have absorbed this book, let's end it with the same exercise from the introduction. Let's see if there's been any change. Find a comfortable place to sit. Close your eyes and take three slow deep breaths. Then think of the word "MONEY." Be honest with yourself about how that makes you feel.
- Do you feel in control of your life?
- Do you feel connected with God, your religion, consciousness, your spirituality, your higher self, or whatever way you see or describe your non-physical self?
- Are you aware how your mind has been programmed to navigate this life?
- To what extent will you embrace and have faith in the system of Capitalism as the storehouse of your savings, accepting the inevitable bouts with *volatility*?
- To what extent can you see how the financial services industry has preyed on your fears of life?
- Can you take steps to remove those fears from your experience, minimize the breaking-news Media, which is all a propaganda machine, and replace them with the voice of your own collaborative team of fiduciary experts for your wealth and well-being solutions?

- To what extent do you feel you are stuck in your circumstances, or do you feel you are a choice-maker and director of your life?
- Are you prepared to make a shift in consciousness and "be"-come the joy inherent to your birthright and to experience the fulfillment of your destiny? If so, now is the time!

Namaste,

Jai

EPILOGUE: OUR LUMINOUS WORK AHEAD UNVEILED

Success is not the key to happiness.
Happiness is the key to success.
—ALBERT SCHWEITZER, GERMAN PHILOSOPHER

I worked with a vice president at a large hospital in North Carolina for a year before my team and I were able to develop a full-scale financial plan for him and his family. We would meet in his executive suite of offices, and he was always late and apologetic for being so. He had files and books neatly stacked on his desk and was always stressed and in a hurry. He confided that he was constantly under pressure from work and even began to reveal financial issues discussed over the family dinner table with his wife. You see, she wanted a vacation home on Martha's Vineyard, and he felt they had no way of affording it. Differences in their respective upbringings played a major role in the discord. This brought a heightened sense of urgency to arrange an overdue planning session with my team and his family, and he reluctantly made time.

As mentioned in this book, at Timonier, the business I founded, we evaluated the financial probabilities of achieving an array of lifestyle paths. We asked that our clients imagined their lives moving through time in the most perfect way. We modeled for them being able to live a kings-and-castles-in-the-sky lifestyle and then tested to see if it was achievable. Then we modeled for a lifestyle that was modest, yet quite fulfilling. In my decades of developing plans for hundreds of families, the vast majority projected achieving a lifestyle somewhere in the middle of these two scenarios. A small percentage of these studies indicated that there needed to be financial adjustments made to achieve an acceptable financial future. And there were a handful of clients who could easily achieve lifestyles beyond their imagined dreams. In final analysis, this couple was one of the financially fortunate outliers of our studies. They were stunned to discover the available possibilities for the journey in front of them.

Unsurprisingly, within a year, a new real estate property on Martha's Vineyard was added to their balance sheet. Soon thereafter, they were blessed to have adopted a child that brought even more meaning and joy into their lives. But the most value that I saw with this work was that it brought peace and harmony to their household. It also brought a centeredness, a balance, a mindfulness to my client who arrived at our subsequent meetings through the years on time, without clutter, and in a state of calm presence for our conversations. It was rewarding to be a part of bringing financial clarity and seeing its effects on the human psyche, emotions, relationships, and experiences. But clarity of financial possibilities and well-managed wealth doesn't always heal the mind and our well-being.

Among the many interesting and beautiful families I worked with through the years, I was fortunate to have worked with a gentleman and his family in Dallas, Texas, whose career culminated in leading an iconic corporation listed on the NYSE. They were among the wealthier families that my team and I had the pleasure of advising. Their complex life situation brought the best out of my team's collaboration, professional expertise, and experience. We radically reduced their cost of professional services and brought financial organization to their entire wealth management framework, from legal to accounting to investment to collections of art to insurance to financial planning and philanthropy. We became their filter for vetting the avalanche of investment and insurance deals that they were constantly bombarded with. My team brought clarity and sophisticated simplicity to their unique life path.

A few years into our relationship, the gentleman fell prey to a debilitating health condition caused by the stresses of his CEO position. It was so traumatic that he soon took early retirement. Even so, he was one of those rare clients of ours who could easily live well beyond his ideal dreams like the family I mentioned above.

Through the ensuing years, financial matters with his adult children created disharmony in his family. Because he found himself with more social and leisure time, he became even more of a target for exotic business adventures, tax avoidance schemes, life insurance and annuity salesmen, and false oracles of economic forecasting. He constantly wrote emails and shared news articles of concerns about market declines as well as rising bull markets. He questioned every sound and carefully designed financial strategy that he'd embraced just years earlier.

I sometimes felt that he was my personal test for remaining centered and untriggered by his stressed behavior. I never attempted to convince him of anything in my communications. I simply restated our principles, the financial facts and economic conditions of the day, illustrated with several appraisals of where he and his family stood in the process of achieving their desired financial goals, and reminded him of his family's lifetime mission statement. We also had many discussions surrounding physical fitness and sports activities, personal interests and pursuits, nutritional regimens, and spirituality. He and his family's participation and communication with our team was fluid and timely, but his inner in-securities were infinitely greater than his outer securities, and he remained stuck in un-serving thought and behavioral patterns for as long as I knew him.

Managing the monetary aspects of family wealth requires a holistic approach. Every segment and every variable of the financial planning equation affects the others. It can sometimes be like solving a Rubik's Cube. Hence, the necessity of working with a team of advisors who are intimately familiar with the details of the family goals and dynamics, are philosophically aligned, and are working from a centralized location for the fiduciary interest of their client.

As you saw with our hospital executive, spending quality time to intentionally develop authentic family life goals with his wealth team of advisors brought organization and clarity to his family's financial matters. It also relieved some of the pressures he absorbed from his work and brought joy and harmony to his household, which led to a more mindful and abundant life.

For many families, even the best of financial circumstances and a team of client-centric wealth advisors aren't enough to stabilize, much less solve, human suffering. As in the case of our Texas CEO, no amount of wealth is going to cure the psyche and emotional storms that this individual will continue to experience. Only a change in consciousness will bring tranquility, joy, and fulfillment to his being. The programming he received from his early years of development will impact his life until he comes face to face with his fears and limitations and connects with his higher self.

We all have the opportunity to live an authentic life chosen for destiny, but we must remove the veils of our inherited and early environments. We must recognize the samskaras, those aspects of our lives that no longer serve us, and peacefully transmute them from our reality. Only then can we begin anew and move into our new reality—one chosen from an authentic heart.

There are many ways to actively remove the behavioral patterns that no longer serve us. These methods will take time and persistent application, but the process is rewarding. The most profound and direct way, the most enriching way, is to know thyself. For to know thyself is to know all of reality. And the only reality is consciousness. Reality is simply the loss of those aspects of ego that do not serve us. This is the doorway to experiencing heaven on earth.

*Step into the fire of self-discovery. This fire will
not burn you, it will only burn what you are not.*
—MOOJI

In co-creation with some amazing partners, I am being led to develop an organization that will change the way we think and feel about money and assist in awakening the god consciousness for all that are ready. We will meet you right where you are. It's time to remove the veils of fear, negative thinking, limiting beliefs, and old paradigms, and reprogram our minds to the destiny we are here to experience that our souls wait patiently for. It's also time to revolutionize and restructure the systems and services that provide support for our one best life journey. The wealth management industry alone cannot do this. Money does not bring lasting happiness to the human condition after a satisfactory base for living has been created.

Consciously developing and preparing the human condition will not only restore peace and contentment to our experience, but it will eliminate the stress and suffering that money can't heal. We are putting together a "quantum living team" that will provide an extraordinary new approach to living that allows us to see our role in life of that of the active creator, rather than just the passive observer, creatively shaping our experience in a conscious and connected universe.

As this book has stated, money doesn't cause stress and suffering; the mind does. Master your mind, and you master your relationship with money and all other relevant categories of your life. In the organization I'm co-creating, we are building a team of advisors and coaches expert in the field of mind, body, and spirit to support our clients and complement the work that our wealth advisory team performs. This entity will be a client-centric team of life advisors operating from a central location we refer to as your Luminous Sanctuary. Our goal is to support the joy inherent as your birthright and enhance your human experience. Our desire is to see your health span equal your life span's longest potential with vitality and abundance.

We are integral beings, and every aspect of our lives affects the others. We understand the intricate web of interconnectedness. Our health impacts our finances and quality of life; our investments impact our taxes, cash flow, government benefits, and retirement; our nutrition impacts our health and how we feel in our body; our relationships impact our emotional state, wealth, and our estate transfer plans; our career impacts our lifestyle, ability to save, and fulfillment to serve; our physical and mental health impacts our cherished relationships and lifespans; and our level of consciousness impacts all that we experience. The fields of wealth and well-being cannot be managed effectively when addressed in fragmentation. It is this merging of Wealth-Care and Mind-Body-Spirit-Care that is our inspired mission at the new organization I'm co-founding. What heals the individual also heals the collective.

So, depending on when you read this book, this may be a pre-opening look to our *integrated quantum living* platform, where we believe that true abundance and fulfillment arise from aligning all aspects of life with our inner wisdom. We understand that financial well-being is just one element of a fulfilling life, which is why we will offer a unique blend of wisdom, wellness, and wealth services that enable individuals to tap into their higher consciousness and achieve holistic well-being.

Our approach will revolve around empowering individuals and families to awaken their consciousness, embrace emotional intelligence, nurture social connections, foster intellectual growth, optimize their esthetic surroundings, adopt health, nutrition, and physical practices leading to a health span that equals an extended life span and to a discovery of occupational gratification that harnesses with clarity and confidence the imagined possibilities of their financial journey. By integrating these vital aspects of life, we will guide our clients towards unlocking their inner wisdom and achieving true self-mastery and balance.

Through the constant feedback loop of client meetings and interactions, I have dedicated my career and profession to improving the human experience. I know without a doubt had the two families mentioned here had access to such a conscious team of professionals and integrated human services, they would have had a more liberated and expanded experience of life and living. One with more ease, grace, harmony, and fulfillment. I feel this body of work will take a quantum leap beyond holistic ... It will be Luminous. See you there!

You may follow our developments at www.LuminousWealth. com, or email me at Tim@LuminousWealth.com.

RESOURCES

Below is a list of websites and books that you may find helpful in your awakening journey of wealth and well-being. The creators of these resources are all devoted masters of their craft. I have benefited greatly from them all.

THE OPTIMIST DAILY

The Optimist Daily is an open-source library of solutions-oriented news stories. They are the antidote to breaking-news Media. A free subscription is available. Of course, a paid subscription is available as well. www.optimistdaily.com.

DR. JOE DISPENZA

A renowned Doctor of Chiropractic, international speaker, author, and teacher, Dr. Joe is a researcher of epigenetics, quantum physics, and neuroscience, who is making an impressionable impact on the world with his mindful meditation techniques where thousands attend his advanced, weeklong retreats. I have experienced Dr. Joe's workshops, read his books, enjoyed his guided meditations, and have been honored with his lecture and guided meditation at the celebration of my company's 20th anniversary. His work is healing and transforming the world, bringing peace and inspiration to everyone's lives he touches. You will oftentimes find me with the Jupiterians Love Brigade in Jupiter, Florida, on Sundays at 6:30 a.m. with a group of geniuses participating in an hour-long walking meditation guided by Dr. Joe's recordings at Marker 24 along the beach. www.drjoedispenza.com.

Additionally, Dr. Joe has taken his teachings at his weeklong retreats to the corporate marketplace where his world class curriculum improves and transforms employees and business development using a unique inside-out reprogramming approach. I experienced his training curriculum and first-class illustrative materials while at Timonier and continue to use these techniques and materials to this day. If you want to improve your company and team performance you may want to contact Julissa Janis, one of Dr. Joe's top gifted corporate consultants/trainers and also co-founder of the Jupiterians Love Brigade. You may review this corporate offering at www.neurochangesolutions.com and, if interested, reach out to Julissa at Julissaj@neurochangesolutions.com.

DR. DEEPAK CHOPRA

After intuitively practicing meditation, sitting on the hearth of my fireplace in my living room in 1997, I gained formal training in primordial sound meditation techniques from Dr. Chopra that I still use daily today. I attended several retreats with Dr. Chopra and his partner, Roger Gabriel, through the years, including a mystical two weeks in India that I've mentioned already in the book. He has a website where you can review offerings for retreats, articles, books, meditation, a well-being app, and more. www.chopra.com.

DR. ALBERTO VILLOLDO

A Cuban-born psychologist, medical anthropologist, professor, author, and founder of Four Winds Society and the Light Body School, Dr. Alberto has discovered a set of technologies that transform the body, heal the soul, and can change the way we live and the way we die. Having studied for over 25 years the shamanic healing practices of the peoples of the Amazon and Andes, he provides courses in self-mastery drawing from the ancient wisdom from these cultures. If you want to taste the perspective of being human from our indigenous earth keepers of wisdom and spirit, you may find what you are looking for at his website. There you will find retreats, books, and online courses for an understanding seldom experienced in our Western culture. I've read his books, including *Grow a New Body*, attended a two-week retreat at his residence in Los Lobos, Chile, and participated in his online courses. One of my favorite quotes from Dr. Alberto is, "Your health span should equal your life span." His teachings for the mind, body, and spirit are invaluable through the lens of light, energy, and vibration. www.thefourwinds.com.

HEARTMATH INSTITUTE

For more than 25 years, HeartMath has been researching the heart-brain connection and learning how the heart influences our perceptions, emotions, intuition, and health. They have recorded the heart to be approximately 60 times greater electrically and up to 5,000 times stronger magnetically than the brain. HeartMath helps you tap into the power and intelligence of your heart and synchronize your emotions with your brain, which awakens you to the best version of yourself. They have several techniques and tools that, once learned, take only minutes a day to implement to relieve stress and anxiety, improve health and wellness, enhance spirituality, and improve your daily human performance. They have a wealth of valuable information on their website, which includes books, courses, training, tools, certifications, and more for both consumers and healthcare professionals. I've experienced their live training courses and use their Inner Balance app for the practice of daily heart coherence, and I find them very impactful in supporting me to experience a balanced, calm, and discerning life. www.heartmath.com.

THE MONROE INSTITUTE

I had read about and followed the Monroe Institute located in Faber, Virginia, for decades but never followed through on enrolling in their on-campus programs. It is known as one of the world's leading education centers for the study of human consciousness. Their founder, Robert Monroe experienced a gifted and most unusual life that you may enjoy reading about one day. He developed a patented hemi-sync process, which synchronizes the two hemispheres of a person's brain, thereby creating a frequency-following response designed to evoke certain effects. The effects include relaxation and sleep induction, learning and memory enhancements, assisting those with physical and mental difficulties, and it can help people reach altered states of consciousness through listening to the sounds of binaural beats, as well as frequency, amplitude, and phase modulation.

About a year ago, I followed through with experiencing one of their short online courses of meditation. I followed up by purchasing their meditation app called Expand. There is a free version of this app, but, of course, I wanted the deep library of options. It's very inexpensive, and it's one of the most enhancing tools that I supplement my meditation practice with. I am able to quiet the mind chatter that initiates many meditations and reach the alpha, theta, and delta levels of awareness with their binaural frequencies embedded in the app's meditations. The Monroe website has an array of individual- and institutional-level programs onsite and online, education, and other outstanding deliverables that you may enjoy in enhancing your daily human experience. www.monroeinstitute.org.

THE WILLFUL WARRIOR

All of life's enlightened masters that I have read about or experienced in person had a dedicated practice of breathwork. Leland Holgate, a combat veteran, has overcome PTSD, addiction, alcoholism, and paralysis from the waist down. He credits his full recovery through natural means with his dedication to meditation, yoga, and ancient breathwork techniques. He has taken his experience of healing and directed it to helping others. Through The Willful Warrior, Leland will teach methods to bring you into new states of consciousness, where the chaos of life fades into the background, and the emotions of bliss, joy, and excitement for the gift of life return to your heart. It brings us to view problems small and large from new perspectives and arrive at different conclusions and solutions. His teachings have become well known and are much sought after. I can personally attest to the benefits of his work as it has awakened a state of wholeness and vibration I've never felt. I have incorporated it into my mindful practice. His website will offer upcoming events and provide videos of his techniques for a subscription fee. Seventy-five percent of net profits are donated to nonprofits and charities that help those in need and evolve the consciousness of the world. www.thewillfulwarrior.org.

THE SOPHIA INSTITUTE

Carolyn Rivers is the founder, director, visionary, and inspiration of the Sophia Institute, serving an international community based in Charleston, South Carolina. Supported by Henk Brandt, her talented husband, author, and mindfulness-based counselor, they have dedicated their lives to offering innovative programs focused on personal and societal transformation. Their mission is to foster the rise of the feminine, in partnership with the masculine, cultivating wisdom, mindfulness, and well-being for a more just, regenerative, spiritually fulfilling, and flourishing world for all people.

They provide forums, retreats, lectures, classes, series, and special events featuring nationally and internationally renowned thought leaders and teachers. They offer programs that are virtual and have online videos, but I would also encourage you to enjoy their programs on location in the beautiful city of Charleston, South Carolina. Speakers such as Dr. Jean Houston, Joan Borysenko, Mark Nepo, and a favorite of mine Carolyn Myss provide information rich in wisdom and healing to our communities and world at large. I've personally been associated with and a supporter of their initiatives and programs through the years. You can browse their impactful work of service at their website. www.thesophiainstitute.org.

HIPPOCRATES WELLNESS

For over 60 years, Hippocrates Wellness has seen practically every illness and disease afflicting humankind pass through their doors. Their world-leading, compassionate team of experts has educated and guided countless lives to optimal health and well-being through nutritional counseling, rejuvenating therapies, ground-breaking lectures and protocols, life-transforming wellness programs, and the Hippocrates' signature nutrient-rich, plant-based organic cuisine.

Whether you want to reverse or prevent ill health, or reset and reboot your whole body, Hippocrates Wellness offers the only ethical and sustainable lifestyle and diet that has been clinically researched consistently for over six decades, providing a unique setting to encourage the reversal of premature aging and disease.

Located in West Palm Beach, Florida, Hippocrates is led by Brian and Anna Maria Clement, both PhDs and LNs, who are the masterminds, stewards, healers, and wisdom keepers for the thousands of patients and clients who have graced their center. I am a graduate of their Reboot Camp Program and can attest to the awe of their offering and holistic healing processes. The scope of describing all they offer is too vast to describe in this summary, so I would encourage you to visit their website. www.hippocrateswellness.org.

LAURA REESE ... A.K.A. LILITH

For those of you who resonate with the knowledge and understanding of energy work through ancient spiritual practices, you may enjoy the unique gifts that Laura provides at Glassroots Energetics. She is a true angel in human form. She is a certified guide, teacher, healer, Kabbalist in the lineage of King Solomon, and celebrates this tradition through offering its healings, teachings, and tools of empowerment to all who are looking for more from life. The healing journey is important to embark on as it returns us to a state of wholeness on all levels: physical, mental, emotional, and spiritual. Through healing we remember who we are and eliminate any behavioral patterns and blockages that stand between us and our true eternal nature. Through her many offerings, Laura will guide you to the level of human and spiritual experience you are seeking. I've benefitted profoundly from her energy work by simply allowing my higher self to stream into my human experience. Her work is provided on location, through retreats, and also remotely. To explore her offerings, you can find her organization at www.glassrootsenergetics.com.

THE WEALTH OF NATIONS, ABRIDGED

The foundation for all modern economic thought and political economy, *The Wealth of Nations* is the magnum opus of Scottish economist Adam Smith, who introduces to the world the very idea of economics and Capitalism in the modern sense of the words. There are five books within this masterpiece. Smith's perspectives are detailed in the following five books: Book I. *Of the Causes of Improvement in the Productive Power of Labour*; Book II. *Of the Nature, Accumulation, and Employment of Stock Introduction*; Book III. *Of the Different Progress of Opulence in Different Nations*; Book IV. *Of Systems of Political Economy*; and Book V. *Of the Revenue of the Sovereign or Commonwealth*. These five books taken together form a giant leap forward in the field of economics.

A product of the Age of Enlightenment, *The Wealth of Nations* is a must-read for all who wish to gain a better understanding of the principles upon which all modern capitalistic economies have been founded and the process of wealth creation that is engendered by those principles. Knowledge is power, and this abridged version will assist you in weathering the daily storms of the Media hysteria about our economy. I have the 1,131-page version but recommend the 150-page abridged version, as I don't want to discourage you from seeking important economic principles.

FACTFULNESS

When asked simple questions about global trends—*what percentage of the world's population lives in poverty, why is the world's population increasing, or how many girls finish school?*—we systematically get the answers wrong. So wrong that a chimpanzee choosing answers at random will consistently outguess teachers, journalists, Nobel laureates, and investment bankers.

In *Factfulness*, professor of international health and global TED phenomenon, Dr. Hans Rosling, together with his two long-time collaborators, Anna Rosling Rönnlund and Ola Rosling, offers a radical new explanation of why this happens. They reveal the ten instincts that distort our perspective—from our tendency to divide the world into two camps (usually some version of "us" and "them") to the way we consume Media (where

135

fear rules) to how we perceive progress (believing that most things are getting worse). Our problem is that we don't know what we don't know, and even our guesses are informed by unconscious and predictable biases.

It turns out that the world, for all its imperfections, is in a much better state than we might think. That doesn't mean there aren't real concerns, but when we worry about everything all the time instead of embracing a worldview based on facts, we can lose our ability to focus on the things that threaten us most.

Inspiring and revelatory, filled with lively anecdotes and moving stories, *Factfulness* is an urgent and essential book that will change the way you see the world and empower you to respond to the crises and opportunities of the future.

Also, I would encourage you to visit www.gapminder.org/ resources and then click on "Understand a Changing World" located in the middle of the page.

SPIRITUAL ECONOMICS

Excerpts from the preface of Eric Butterworth's *Spiritual Economics* read:

> Ours is an age of great change. Great corporations are streamlining their workforce to reflect the need for greater efficiency and the impact of automation. Whole industries are being eliminated or are transitioning to new fields of service. Jobs are being eliminated and many workers need to undergo retraining for entry into new fields of endeavor. There is a great need to establish ourselves in those things that are conducive to prosperity. We need to turn the focus of our attention away from lack, layoffs, and limitations and on to the omnipresence of universal substance. Just as there are experiences that are healthful to us, so are their experiences that are "wealthful." Expose yourself constantly to wealthful ideas—think prosperity, think substance, think affluence. Your life will be influenced for good or ill by the kinds of thoughts that rule your mind and manifest in your world. Spiritual Economics is all about such thoughts. I strongly recommend it to you.

And supported by the testimony of scores of people who have written to tell of the positive influence on their lives of working with this book, I sincerely believe it can be a wealthful influence in your life.

You can analyze the world economy, politics, social structures, and the changing winds of time, but nothing will change your mental and emotional state with this higher perspective. This non-theological approach has assisted me in staying centered during the most difficult times of economic uncertainty and chaos. It's been a guidepost for my perspective of life and living for many years.

BREAKING THE HABIT OF BEING YOURSELF

You are not doomed by your genes and hardwired to be a certain way for the rest of your life. A new science is emerging that empowers all human beings to create the reality they choose. In *Breaking the Habit of Being Yourself*, renowned author, speaker, researcher, and chiropractor Dr. Joe Dispenza combines the fields of quantum physics, neuroscience, brain chemistry, biology, and genetics to show you what is truly possible.

Not only will you be given the necessary knowledge to change any aspect of yourself, you will also be taught the step-by-step tools to apply what you learn in order to make measurable changes in any area of your life. Dr. Joe demystifies ancient understandings and bridges the gap between science and spirituality. Through his powerful workshops and lectures, thousands of people in 24 different countries have used these principles to change from the inside out. Once you break the habit of being yourself and truly change your mind, your life will never be the same. This book can easily be found on Dr. Joe's website or on Amazon.

SIMPLE WEALTH INEVITABLE WEALTH—20TH ANNIVERSARY EDITION

Nick Murray is an advisor to advisors and has been a valuable colleague throughout my career with his enlightening lectures and monthly writings. He holds light when the world is in darkness and resonance and order when there is chaos and disorder. He is a master of his discipline and a Shakespeare with his expressions. In this book, he establishes two complementary investing truths: (1) that equities are essential to long-term wealth-building and to a solidly rising income in retirement; and (2) that no one will ever be able to hold equities through all the fears (fads and new paradigms) of the market cycle without an empathetic but toughloving behavioral investment counselor. Even Jack Nicklaus and Tiger Woods needed swing coaches and sports psychologists.

This wonderful, easy-to-read book, which you'll want to philosophically adopt for your family and beyond, presents:

- That real wealth—an income one doesn't outlive and a significant legacy to one's heirs—can only be achieved through a program of lifetime equity investing.
- That mainstream equities historically create lifetime retirement income which rises through time at a significant premium to consumer inflation.
- That the achievement of real wealth in equities is not driven by investment "performance" but by investor behavior—making a lifetime plan and sticking to it, ignoring both bull market fads and bear market panic capitulation.
- That, in practice, no one will ever be able to resist the great behavioral traps of equity investing without a high-quality advisor.
- That the highest, best, and most valuable function of an advisor is guiding clients past The Big Mistake, in all of its many manifestations.

FAMILY WEALTH—KEEPING IT IN THE FAMILY

Every family, looking at the next generation, hopes to confer advantages that are more than just material and financial—to inculcate character and leadership, to inspire creativity and enterprise, to help all family members find and follow their individual callings, and to avoid the financial dependency and *loss* of initiative that can all too often be an unwanted consequence of financial success. Yet many families never succeed in realizing that vision, much less sustaining it for three, four, or five generations and beyond.

James Hughes, the author of *Family Wealth—Keeping It in the Family*, has thought deeply about these challenges, and his insights are at once practical and profound. For more than three decades, he has personally guided multiple generations of families in creating strategies to preserve their human and intellectual capital as well as their financial assets. His teachings synthesize insights from psychology, anthropology, political history, philosophy, economic theory, and the law, with examples ranging from Aristotle to cutting-edge social science theory.

This landmark book has changed the way exceptional families think about their heritage, their wealth, and their legacy to future generations—and while I haven't yet acquired it—is now revised and expanded.

I embody in my viewpoints a favorite quote from James Hughes:

> Every family I have observed that is successfully preserving its wealth is a reflection of the five virtues of truth, beauty, goodness, community, and compassion. Transcending all of these is its reflection of love. Families who preserve their wealth successfully reflect these virtues in their relationships both with family members and with all persons outside the family. I am convinced that without this spiritual component, a family cannot succeed in preserving itself, since its value system will fail and with that failure will come its disintegration.

And so will a nation. We must restore and awaken our spiritual connection, whatever that looks like, within each one of us.

ACKNOWLEDGMENTS

F OR OVER 39 YEARS, I journeyed the field of wealth management as my laboratory in witnessing and understanding the human experience of the individuals, families, and institutions I humbly served. I followed my divine guidance and years of research to develop the processes and professional teams to bring clarity, organization, fulfillment, and prosperity to many wonderful and extraordinary clients. They were not only clients, but they also invited me into their lives as family, where all of life's disappointments, sorrows, fears, resilience, triumphs, joy, and love are openly shared unashamedly. I was both the teacher and the student in witness of these cherished experiences. It is with this journey that *The Awakened Investor* has been realized. I have altered the names, genders, occupations, and locations of the individuals mentioned in the book to protect their privacy. So, I want to give my heartfelt gratitude to all those families that I have served without naming them to honor their confidentiality.

I was blessed to receive a great deal of high-quality assistance in the production of this book. I want to give special thanks to Sean Donahue and Andrew Palmer for the countless hours helping me organize and shape the content with three-way calls from all parts of the United States. I want to give my gratitude to Brett Hilker for guiding me to the conclusion of this book with his authorship insights and recommendations. One of those recommendations led me to the talented Nancy Pile who provided editorial mastery and suggestions to bring this message to its final and best presentation. Additionally, I thank Julie Ann Ehrenzweig, Nancy's trusted colleague and collaborator, for her final editing and proofreading.

I want to recognize Hugh Massie for lending his valuable time, attention, encouragement and writing the Forward to the words in this book. I also want to thank and acknowledge Hugh's colleague, Leon Morales, for his dedication to the work of DNA Behavior and sharing his expertise of the human psyche and identifying opportunities for healing the human condition. Thank you, Julissa Janis, for your review time and creative input between your travels around the world serving to raise consciousness. Julissa is also credited with manifesting the title of this book. She downloaded the name from her higher self over coffee in Jupiter. And finally, I want to give my appreciation to Janet Edwards for her suggestions at the conclusion of this work and mostly for the inspiration she gave me to finish.

ABOUT THE AUTHOR

TIM "JAI" BAKER, CIMA®, GFS® is a steadfast visionary and founder of Timonier Family Office, Ltd. serving multi-generational families, retirement plans, and endowments in Winston Salem, North Carolina. He developed a pioneering philosophy that wealth management works best when it's tightly integrated with personal well-being and firmly grounded in lifelong, positive relationships. For nearly four decades, Tim worked with  hundreds of high-net-worth families, corporate retirement plans, endowments, trusts, and medical hospitals. His holistic approach mandated having a team of multi-disciplinary professional advisors working from a centralized location in order to carry out the mission statement of the families his company served.

Having turned over the reins of Timonier to his professional colleagues, Tim is now in the birthing stages of a company that will fully awaken the consumer to their higher self as they consciously make choices for a luminous life—one that sheds the environmental history that no longer serves our human experience, that makes dormant the reactionary systems and beliefs of the reptilian mind, and replaces it with conscious software directing an authentic limitless version of the quantum species humans are on the verge to becoming.

You will be able to stay in resonance with Tim's developments via his website www.LuminousWealth.com. His email is Tim@LuminousWealth.com.

Made in United States
Orlando, FL
30 November 2024